A Levinasian Ethics for Education's Commonplaces

The Cultural and Social Foundations of Education

Series Editor: **A.G. Rud**, Distinguished Professor in the College of Education of Washington State University, USA.

The Palgrave Pivot series on the Cultural and Social Foundations of Education seeks to understand educational practices around the world through the interpretive lenses provided by the disciplines of philosophy, history, sociology, politics, and cultural studies. This series focuses on the following major themes: democracy and social justice, ethics, sustainability education, technology, and the imagination. It publishes the best current thinking on those topics, as well as reconsideration of historical figures and major thinkers in education.

Titles include:

Clarence W. Joldersma
A LEVINASIAN ETHICS FOR EDUCATION'S COMMONPLACES
Between Calling and Inspiration

palgrave▶pivot

A Levinasian Ethics for Education's Commonplaces: Between Calling and Inspiration

Clarence W. Joldersma
Professor of Education, Calvin College, USA

palgrave
macmillan

A LEVINASIAN ETHICS FOR EDUCATION'S COMMONPLACES
Copyright © Clarence W. Joldersma, 2014.

All rights reserved.

First published in 2014 by
PALGRAVE MACMILLAN®
in the United States—a division of St. Martin's Press LLC,
175 Fifth Avenue, New York, NY 10010.

Where this book is distributed in the UK, Europe and the rest of the world, this is by Palgrave Macmillan, a division of Macmillan Publishers Limited, registered in England, company number 785998, of Houndmills, Basingstoke, Hampshire RG21 6XS.

Palgrave Macmillan is the global academic imprint of the above companies and has companies and representatives throughout the world.

Palgrave® and Macmillan® are registered trademarks in the United States, the United Kingdom, Europe and other countries.

ISBN: 978-1-137-41551-6 EPUB
ISBN: 978-1-137-41549-3 PDF
ISBN: 978-1-137-42916-2 Hardback

Library of Congress Cataloging-in-Publication Data is available from the Library of Congress.

A catalogue record of the book is available from the British Library.

First edition: 2014

www.palgrave.com/pivot

DOI: 10.1057/9781137415493

To John and Nick

Contents

Series Editor's Preface	viii
Preface and Acknowledgments	x
Introduction	1
1 Calling and Inspiration	**7**
Transcendence	9
Calling	12
Inspiration	16
2 Learning	**22**
The student as autonomous	24
The inspired subject	28
The asymmetry of learning	31
Inspiration for learning	34
The call to responsibility animating justice	40
3 Teaching	**43**
The teacher as autonomous	44
The responsible subject	47
The asymmetry of teaching	49
Called to teach	52
The inspiration to hope animating justice	58
4 Curriculum	**61**
Curriculum as representational knowledge	62
Unsuspected horizons for representations	65
Beyond representational knowledge	73
Calling and inspiration in the curriculum	81

5 Institutions	89
The limits of institutionalization	90
From ethics to justice	97
Justice in institutions	101
Educating for justice	105
Conclusion	112
References	118
Index	122

Series Editor's Preface

A major theme for this series in the cultural and social foundations of education is how educational practices and institutions develop or hinder an ethical stance of care for others and the planet. Clarence Joldersma's *A Levinasian Ethics for Education's Commonplaces: Between Calling and Inspiration* considers the commonplaces of schooling—the student, teacher, curriculum, and institution – afresh through the lens of the ethics of Emmanuel Levinas. Joldersma sees an animating ethical orientation grounded in the primordial relationship of humans to each other as the difference in education for human flourishing versus simply training or preparing students for the world of work and commerce. For Joldersma, education is ethical development. For him all other instrumentalities in education, such as gaining knowledge for career preparation, would be deficient because they do not originate nor are they continually informed and shaped by an ethical orientation. Education calls for a complete turn toward the care of the other and this planet. As we grow and learn about the world, we may witness suffering in the world due to hunger and other dangers. We may respond to this suffering, ignore it, or worse, abet its growth. What causes us to move from willful ignorance to action oriented toward the suffering other? For Joldersma, a Levinasian orientation calls and inspires us toward a set of actions and attitudes by which we respond to the ills of others and the planet.

Joldersma's revision of educational commonplaces is fresh and challenges currently accepted wisdom. He sees the ideal student as not simply the autonomous, self-regulated learner, but one who is vitally connected to the teacher as other, the teacher who calls to that student to heed the needs of others around him or her. The curriculum is not a total and compartmentalized map of knowledge, for that belies the mystery of what we know and how we know it. Joldersma notes that Levinas makes room here for listening and openness to that which is beyond the curriculum. At a time when teachers continue to be attacked for supposed deficiencies of knowledge and skill, Joldersma puts even more responsibility on the teacher, who is there as the other to the student, and thus a constant perturbation to classroom stasis and complacency. Teaching here cannot simply be transmission of knowledge, nor can it be simply characterized by the support of critical thinking or problem-solving. For Joldersma, the teacher has a larger responsibility as the other who calls the student out beyond the classroom to witness the imperfect world, to inspire that student to strive toward aiding others and showing reverence for our fragile planet.

In this important book, education occurs when one is called to go beyond school walls to the world outside, and to consider injustice, lack of care, and cruelty, where one can be inspired by hope that the world can become a better, more just, more tolerant, and kinder place. This is all the more important, as Joldersma notes, in our world today, where education has been largely evacuated not only of its normative function, but also of its connection to that primordial and elemental relationship we have to one another, to non-human animals, to plant life, and to our planet. I urge you to read this timely and provocative volume in this series as you consider how you are called or not, inspired or not, by what goes on in the world, especially as it connects to schooling for social and planetary justice.

Preface and Acknowledgments

The idea for this book first arose over a decade ago, in 2003, while I was editing a volume of essays by Nicholas Wolterstorff entitled *Educating for Shalom* (2004) and at the same time trying to understand the dense prose of Levinas's texts. I had just been chosen as one of the ARIHE (Association of Reformed Institutions of Higher Education) Lecturers for 2003–2005, for which I needed to prepare three lectures on philosophical perspectives in education. I combined Wolterstorff's passion for justice with Levinas's insight about ethical intersubjectivity in writing about the purpose of education as well as on the commonplaces of learning, teaching, and the curriculum. These lectures formed the centerpiece of an emerging book manuscript. Wolterstorff's focus on social justice and Levinas's insight in rethinking human subjectivity as an ethical relation intersected in my struggle to turn these lectures into a book. I reworked this manuscript many times, allowing it to languish on multiple occasions, yet returning to it time and again. In some ways to my surprise, what has emerged over the many years and multiple drafts is my own voice.

There are number of people I would like to thank, for without them this book would likely not have seen the light of day. I thank Ruth Groenhout and Nel Noddings for encouraging me to pursue my Levinas interest; Gert Biesta for his multiple conversations with me about Levinas and education; Darren Walhof for his many insightful suggestions and close readings of parts of this manuscript and its ideas over the years. I also thank Maria Cimitile, Henry

Luttikhuizen, Matt Walhout, David Billings, Lambert Zuidervaart, Ann Chinnery, Sharon Todd, Denise Egéa-Kuehne, Paul Standish, and Barb Stengel for their encouragement of my scholarship. Finally, I thank my life partner and spouse Grace Veldhuisen Joldersma for her gracious and unfailing support for all my projects, including particularly this book.

palgrave▸pivot

www.palgrave.com/pivot

Introduction

Abstract: *The introduction sets the stage by introducing the difference between education and schooling, and between Levinas's idea of ethics and other uses of the term. It explains the purpose of the book as an extended critique of schooling as currently imagined, especially in a globalizing age. It concludes with a brief overview of each chapter.*

Keywords: ethics; neoliberalism; schooling

Joldersma, Clarence W. *A Levinasian Ethics for Education's Commonplaces: Between Calling and Inspiration.* New York: Palgrave Macmillan, 2014. DOI: 10.1057/9781137415493.0004.

Formal schooling is a pervasive part of society in many countries. At its best it contributes positively to the social fabric and dynamics of public life. At its worst, it reinforces pernicious inequalities and wastes precious time and resources, detracting from sustainable flourishing. The difference between these two could be thought of as the presence or absence of education, something that emerges when a particular ethical orientation animates schooling. Attending to the ethical current that ought to run through formal schooling is crucial not only for the institutions themselves but also for sustainable flourishing more generally. What is the ethical orientation that ought to direct formal schooling, allowing education to emerge? How might we typify the ethical orientation that gives rise to education in the context of formal schooling? My project is to make visible an ethical current that ought to orient formal schooling, including particularly high school and undergraduate institutions. My focus is on the commonplaces of school: teaching, learning, the curriculum, and the milieu (Schwab, 1978), devoting a chapter to each of them.

A particular idea of ethics runs through the book. The question of ethics in schooling might be depicted as a duty to treat each student fairly, for example by rewarding them according to academic merit, rather than based on another scheme, such as good looks, or gender, or race. On this construal, treating each student ethically means treating each of them with the respect they deserve. Or, school ethics might be portrayed as a set of specific student behaviors, that is, the realm of personal morality, including honesty, industriousness, compliance with rules, and civility toward others. Academically, ethics is often construed as a specialized study within the realm of philosophy. Under this description, we can identify different and competing sets of ethical theories, such as deontological, consequentialist, and care-theory approaches.

In this book I will be using the term *ethics* in a different manner. Following Emmanuel Levinas, I use the term to indicate an original, primary relation to another human. Rather than an alternative to consequentialist or deontological theories, I will be using *ethics* to indicate an original condition that marks the intersubjective relation between two persons. In a sentence, ethics marks my non-totalizing relation with the other person, characterized by a call to responsibility and an inspiration to hope. From a first-person perspective, the relation to the other is asymmetric. This notion of ethics will run as a subterranean current in subsequent chapters.

By drawing on Levinas's notion of the ethical, my intent is to unsettle the notion that education is present by default wherever modern institutionalization and organization of formal schooling occur, especially in today's neoliberal climate where schooling's aim seems to be producing disciplined and docile economic bodies ready to be cogs in the world economy (Tuschling, & Engemann, 2006). My idea is that education emerges when schooling aligns itself more clearly with the primordial ethical modes of being human. Education is not ethically neutral, but it involves an original ethical relation to other human beings. In particular, when an ethical condition orients schooling's commonplaces—learning, teaching, curriculum, and institutions—then education can emerge. My approach thus argues against viewing education as merely a function of preparing students for the economic system. Rather, education emerges as a response to the call of justice, something that forms a ubiquitous, if often unacknowledged, horizon for social life. Schooling ought to be animated by a primordial ethical relation.

My goal is to align formal schooling more explicitly with the ethical. The book is, therefore, an extended critique of schooling as society currently imagines it. More positively, redirecting schooling through an ethical understanding of what orients its commonplaces implicitly calls schools to be oriented toward the vulnerable in society and around the globe. For schooling to be oriented by the ethical is to structure into its very institution a focus toward those who suffer and who have no voice of their own. Ethics reorients schooling in its attempts to making positive contributions to the public good of society.

This is more important now than ever, in the twenty-first century. As the forces of globalization change not only national economies but also individual lives, as wars on terrorism dominate the news, as the gap between rich and poor is widening, as economies bifurcate in reaction to self-serving and powerful corporate interests, it is increasingly important to think about education as oriented ethically and toward justice. Schooling, especially in an age of measurement (Biesta, 2010), has a difficult time acknowledging that society is filled with pain, suffering, and woundedness, and that the earth currently is precarious in its support of biotic, including human, life. Although the earth is still a generous support for life, and society has much goodness, often schooling does not acknowledge the context of the earth's precariousness and the world's tears of suffering. As a uniquely situated social institution, schooling needs to be oriented to the call for justice. Some might argue that attempting to be the best school system in the world, as measured by standardized testing, constitutes this orientation. Then ensuring students to be the best in the world at math and science is a concrete way of saying that education is socially just. However, this argument falls short. The social contexts of schools centrally includes the call of justice that is embodied in the hunger of those who go often without food, the struggle of those who search for jobs that do not seem to exist for them, the pain of those who are abandoned by the world to refugee camps, the poverty reflected in the squalor of many American inner cities, the ailments caused by pollution in our modern industrial products, the peril felt by those who are not accepted by their communities, the destruction caused by civil strife around the world, the danger of working conditions in sweatshops that produce disposable consumer goods for the rich, the increasing difference between the rich and poor, and the devastation of gays and lesbians forced out of home communities. Schooling oriented by the call of justice recognizes itself as situated in these realities and understands itself as having to do with human flourishing in local communities and around the globe, precisely because there is so much suffering and pain, hardship and oppression. Schooling shaped by the call of justice interprets the teacher, the student, the curriculum, and the institution as oriented by the ethical. In what follows, I develop the ethical orientation that animates each of these commonplaces.

In Chapter 1, I articulate Levinas's idea of the ethical as the structural call to responsibility for the other's good. I first develop an idea of transcendence, especially as relates to what I term 'time immemorial' and 'time unforeseen.' I concretize this by elaborating two types of indirect experiences, one that I name *call* and the other that I refer to as *inspiration*. My goal is to interpret education's commonplaces in light of these two experiences. I argue that these form the structural conditions of those commonplaces, namely, being called to normative responsibility and being inspired with a hope that motivates to action. The idea of a regulative function uncovers the ethical orientation that gives rise to education.

In Chapter 2, I re-situate our understanding of the student and learning. By recasting the student's subjectivity in terms of a deep relation to the teacher as other, I suggest that the learning process involves welcoming an external disturbance, something I interpret as the inspirational nature of what Levinas calls the ethical. This situates and relativizes the traditional model of the student as autonomous self-learner. The Levinasian notion involves interpreting human subjectivity radically as intersubjective, in terms of inspiration, which comes through the teacher.

Chapter 3 addresses teaching and the teacher in a similar fashion. I situate my Levinasian framework in terms of the teacher's subjectivity, traditionally construed as an autonomous subject embodying rationally developed disciplinary knowledge. Below that autonomy, the subjectivity of the teacher is a call to responsibility that comes through the student other, that is, as a unique person. This call acts as a regulatory function that appears as a structural responsibility for the teacher.

In Chapter 4, I address the curriculum. I situate the representational model of knowledge typically connected to our understanding of curricular content within a Levinasian frame. My analysis suggests that the representational model is inadequate for understanding curricular knowledge, and supplements it with the Levinasian ideas of listening and tactful touch. These concepts unsettle the perception of a finished character of the knowledge associated with the curriculum and its concomitant compartmentalization into the disciplines. My reinterpretation invites seeing curriculum as truthful disclosure of the world in ways beyond representation and gives the teacher a function of trusteeship. This analysis follows Levinas's suspicion of totalizing understanding of curriculum, unsettling its disciplinary confinement and encyclopedic comprehension.

In Chapter 5, I address the institutional character of education. Here a Levinasian framework reveals that institutionalization is both a limitation on, and a concretization of, positively valorized educational experiences. In particular, my analysis shows that formal organization is an important avenue for discharging its ethical obligations in a responsible manner while simultaneously imposing restrictions on such possibilities. Because of the way that organization of educational practices occurs, ethics and justice as regulative conditions turn out to have a disruptive character. This alternative perspective reveals that while formal schooling is irreplaceable as a way to respond to the ethical call to responsibility, orienting action toward justice, it is also continually disrupted in that response by the same conditions that make it possible.

I conclude with a short chapter that brings together these ethical orientations. There I reiterate that education emerges most fully when schooling's every-day activities do not stay within the walls of school. Rather, education breaks out when schools respond positively to being called to take responsibility for the world's vulnerable and to being inspired to hope that things can get better. That is, education emerges when schooling's ethical orientation is ultimately animated by the call of justice that comes from the world.

1
Calling and Inspiration

Abstract: *This chapter develops Levinas's idea of the ethical as the structural call to responsibility for the other's good. I first develop an idea of transcendence, especially as relates to what I term 'time immemorial' and 'time unforeseen.' I concretize this by elaborating two types of indirect experiences, one that I name* call *and the other that I refer to as* inspiration. *My goal is to interpret education's commonplaces in light of these two experiences. I argue that these form the structural conditions of those commonplaces, namely, being called to normative responsibility and being inspired with a hope that motivates to action. The idea of a regulative function uncovers the ethical orientation that gives rise to education.*

Keywords: calling; ethics; hope; normativity; transcendence

Joldersma, Clarence W. *A Levinasian Ethics for Education's Commonplaces: Between Calling and Inspiration.* New York: Palgrave Macmillan, 2014. DOI: 10.1057/9781137415493.0005.

The stated purpose of formal schooling has changed over time. Earlier, many argued that its role was to develop citizens who could actively participate in democratic society or to provide economic opportunities for upward mobility. In the past thirty years, the stated purpose has shifted to efficiently creating workers for the global economy. There are myriads of structural features associated with current formal schooling. Teaching is almost always done in the context of large groups of students, whose differences are only indirectly acknowledged and who are treated as if they were virtually identical. Learning takes place in the context of other learners who are attempting to learn the same thing at the same time. The curriculum is most often organized around subjects, units roughly based on academic disciplines or on material thought to be important for entry into those disciplines. Formal assessment is ubiquitous in institutionalized schooling, which currently has a heavy emphasis on high-stakes standardized testing.

The recent era of high-stakes testing can rightly be called an age of measurement (Biesta, 2010). In this interpretation, the purpose of schooling is translated into quantifiable outcomes, where a school's primary purpose is considered to be ensuring that the majority of students reach proficiency in various basic subjects as measured on standardized tests. On this model, learning is equated with short-term acquisition of testable basic skills and knowledge, and teaching is depicted as ensuring that such skills and information be learned. The curriculum is the material constituting the content of such learning and teaching. And schooling's institutional structure is modeled as formal supervision, including hierarchical lines of accountability, for such teaching and learning. The schooling mechanism itself is thought to be the proper and primary vehicle to deliver 'shovel ready' workers for a national economy to compete in a global context.

I aim to unsettle this understanding of schooling. I believe this current orientation has lost its educational moorings. My goal is to reorient schooling by suggesting it needs to be more explicitly animated by an ethical undercurrent—only then will education emerge. For this, I would like to use Emmanuel Levinas's understanding of ethics, something I develop in some detail in this chapter. I first explore the idea of transcendence, and then develop the ideas of calling and inspiration. These concepts will be used in the subsequent chapters.

Transcendence

The ethical is a call to responsibility and an inspiration to hope. Both of these reorient the self-centered preoccupation of striving to live. In the context of society, the ethical is felt as something implicit that regulates social life. The idea of a regulative function uncovers an ethical normativity and animation that relativizes, if not undermines, the centrality of the self-centered character of one's striving to live.

To sketch this out more fully requires a discussion about transcendence. Although not without some risk, I will employ the idea of *transcendent condition* throughout the book. Transcendence is an incoming movement from some 'beyond,' something that shows up as an "affective disruption" within one's subjectivity (Bergo, 2005, pp. 142–143). Transcendence is a dynamic, directional relation between me and something that is not me, where something *outside* oneself is experienced as a disruption *within*. The disruptive movement is felt simultaneously within and outside, an experience of something coming in while simultaneously being pulled toward it, something strange that is, nevertheless, deeply personal.

What is transcendent is not easily captured, either conceptually or experientially, as we experience transcendence *indirectly*. Bergo's idea of affective disruption is a good term for its indirect character. Affective disruption shows up particularly in two phenomena: normativity and hope. By normative I mean, rather than usual or average, the experience of an *ought*—how we *ought* to live. From this vantage point, transcendence is experienced as something incoming that disrupts our satisfaction with status quo practices, experienced as a pull that things ought to be different. But the incoming disruption is simultaneously felt as if it comes from somewhere deep within. It is felt as a personal disruption of satisfaction with the status quo, encountered as a gap between the way things are and how they should be. It is felt as a personal obligation to close that gap while simultaneously feeling that the gap is unbridgeable.

This leads to a second affective disruption, accompanying the first, an experience of *hope*. Despite the felt roadblocks and obstacles—the experience of unbridgeable gaps between the way things are and how they ought to be—humans, nevertheless, also often experience an inner conviction that maintains a positive outlook, an experience we rightly identify as hope. Hope is the conviction that overcoming impossibilities is possible, despite the odds.

The felt disruptions I'm identifying as normativity and hope are complex affects that implicate each other. Together, the obligation felt as the normative *ought* is simultaneously sensed as a hope in a *real possibility* of the impossible. I'm suggesting that normativity and hope each brings in the other while simultaneously keeping the other at a distance. This dynamic of separation and connection indicates a trace of something transcendent.

Normativity and hope are not neutral disruptions. Normativity provides the basis for critique of society. What makes it possible to criticize society's inequalities is a normative understanding of what the good life ought to be. Normativity is felt as how we ought to live, individually as well as collectively. That oughtness provides the traction for critique of how things are. Normativity functions as a vantage point from which to identify the fault lines in the organization of present society and its institutionalized practices. At the same time, hope provides the necessary traction for attempting to do the concrete work necessary to bring about positive change in society. Hopefulness provides the necessary impetus to move society against its current dynamics of how things are, to how they ought to be. The hopeful dimension thus functions as a counterforce to the causal powers that maintain the status quo. Critique and action form an indissoluble tandem, informed by the affective disruptions of normativity and hope.

The felt disruptions of normativity and hope are experiences of transcendence. But, as *transcendence*, we experience them only indirectly, as traces. To highlight the 'trace' character, I will use the notions of calling and inspiration. We experience 'the ought' of normativity as being *called* to something, and we experience the possibility of hope as being *inspired* by something. Calling and inspiration are indirect, enigmatic experiences. More specifically, as calling and inspiration, these are experiences of simultaneous presence and absence, as something lacking while something is here, identifying that which is and that which ought to come about. I thus use the terms call and inspiration to mark felt experiences as traces, not fully present.

The enigmatic character of call and inspiration can be brought out more clearly by connecting them to the idea of time. The phenomena of past and future mark something as simultaneously absent and present. I'm connecting *call* to something experienced in the present as coming from a time past and *inspiration* to something also experienced in the present, but coming to us from a future time.

Now, this has some risk. Talk of the past can be construed as an actual past, one that used to be present, a known historical period, one that is remembered. And we might infuse that memory with a kind of normativity, namely, as an Edenic time in which all things were right and beautiful, something for which we should rightly pine. Similarly talk of the future can equally be construed as an actual historical period, say, in fifty years, or after the revolution. And we might infuse that actual future as some better time which we can concretely envision. There is, of course, nothing wrong with pining for an actual past time when things were remembered as better. Similarly, there is much to be said for envisioning an actual future in which things will be better. But these are the "present past" and the "present future" (Caputo, 2012). We can use the terms memory and vision as placeholders, in the present, to refer to these two. Although memories are about the past, they are not themselves in the past—they are totally present to us, individually or collectively, in the present. We might say that they are present representations of the past, bringing the past to mind in the present. Similarly, although visions are about the future, they are not in the future—they also are totally present to us in the present. We might say that they are present representations of the future, bringing the future to mind in the present. Or, to put it slightly differently, our present living, here and now, is lived in the context of present memories and present visions. However, these do not depict the enigmatic character of call and inspiration.

The felt call to normativity is something that comes from beyond present memory, something that I will depict with the phrase 'a time immemorial.' And I will depict the felt inspiration to hope, as something that comes from beyond present vision, by using the phrase 'a time unforeseen.' Both of these are meant to signal something enigmatic, namely, not recoverable into memory and not projectable into vision. When we look back in the past, a time immemorial refers to something located in a time that cannot be brought adequately into present memory. And when we look into the future, a time unforeseeable refers to something located in a time that cannot be adequately envisioned as a concrete future. Together, these two form transcendent conditions for the present.

These conditions, felt as the enigmatic traces of calling and inspiration, animate and orient action here and now, on this globe, in this society, in the twenty-first century. Something *calls* us here and now not just to sit on our hands waiting around for some perfect society. Something *inspires* us here and now to work to such ends, even though they are difficult if not next to impossible. I will explore each of these in more detail.

Calling

In this section I will explore more fully the enigmatic experience of transcendence I am naming the call of normativity and connecting it to what I'm calling ethics. By relating normativity to the idea of a time immemorial I will explore the conditioning character of the ethical.

Levinas uses the phrase "a time immemorial" to suggest an opening onto mystery (Levinas, 1987, p. 80). The idea of a time immemorial is a temporal metaphor for the mystery of how and why something exists. By mystery I mean a reality that is not self-sufficient, something that does not carry on its sleeve its own story of existence. The phrase creates conceptual room for the idea that the process of coming-into-existence leaves little cognitive trace in the subsequent newly minted existent. There seems to be no obvious, self-contained, easily found evidence of the movement of coming–into-existence that can be garnered from the resultant order and structures. More strongly, the notion of a time immemorial fundamentally involves the idea of coming to be seemingly out of nowhere (Levinas, 2001a, p. 75).

Levinas suggests that the mystery of existence essentially involves being called—called into being. That is, existence is not first the concrete existent thing itself. The mystery of existence is precisely the fact that a thing, structure, or process—including trees, stars, dogs, atoms, laws, social structures, economic systems—*isn't* itself because of itself. It is what it is not from its own internal dynamics, but because it is *called* into being from elsewhere, external to itself.

The idea of being called in general doesn't yet fully illuminate this call's enigmatic character. Lots of calls successfully register through our auditory equipment, ones that we can hear quite clearly, both their character as call and their particular content. Auditory calls in and of themselves are not any more mysterious than visual intuitions. By contrast, there is something essentially enigmatic about the particular call associated with existence, something that cannot be recovered into memory. It is this that the negative prefix 'a time *im*memorial' indicates.

The trope 'a time immemorial' is meant to indicate a sequence: first comes the call and then the response. The mystery of existence is a primordial response that comes *after* the call. From an existent's perspective, the response is primordial, the first thing, although, as a response, it responds to a call that came before. The mysteriousness of existence is that something answers a call before it seems rightly able to do so. More strongly, central to being an existent is precisely not to exist when answering the call to come into existence. In order to come into existence a call must be answered obediently (Levinas, 1998d, p. 113).

For this reason I'm characterizing the call in temporal terms. The trope 'obedience before existence' is a way of speaking about the call from a time immemorial. For a call to be recoverable into memory, the existent must exist at the time of the call; but if the call happens to bring it into existence, then the call exists prior to the possibility of bringing it to mind. Hence the call is from beyond memory. This 'time' of the call, the 'time' of obedience before existence, can best be indicated rather than explained; the trope 'time immemorial' attests to a mystery rather than explaining it. I put 'time' in scare quotes to signal that it isn't temporal in our usual sense, of an actual time in the past that used to be present. The call that can never be brought into presence is an enigma. Only the history of existing reality—that which once was present but slipped into the past—is a candidate for present memories, for being represented in the present *as* a memory. The very 'essence' of obedience before existence is beyond memory, situated in a time immemorial (Levinas, 1998c, p. 97).

Obedience to the call is not an *autonomous* affirmation, as if it were one option among others freely chosen. Instead, the response is the acquiescence of submission (Levinas, 1998d, p. 122)—the response of affirmation is a kind of passivity. It is the passivity of being affirmative before being ready to reasonably discern what is being submitted to. The passivity of an existent called into being while not being there to hear the call, but which it, nevertheless, affirms, is what Levinas calls pure passivity (Levinas, 1996, p. 89). The passivity of affirmation answers the call from a time immemorial without bringing it into memory, without being able to recover the call into the present.

What is felt as an affective disruption is the trace of the call from a time immemorial. The experienced normative character of the trace is a felt responsibility, one reorienting thoughts and actions, which comes from elsewhere. By coming from a time immemorial, the call's content is not recoverable into adequate representations; rather, the normativity is experienced as intruding into our subjectivity before we are ready, asking for our affirmation before we are in a position to make adequate judgments about it. This creates the orienting character of normativity, uncovering the 'ought' of responsibility prior to our freedom as autonomous subjects.

The normativity of the call is asymmetric. The asymmetry of the normative oughtness shows itself as an obligation beyond our voluntary commitments and judgments. More strongly, it *forces* us into becoming responsible beings, beyond our minds or wills, by disrupting ourselves as centered, conscious subjects. The normativity of the call is experienced as an imperative obligation that *seeps into* our consciousness before we are totally aware of it. Before we can theorize about it, grasp it in our consciousness, model it intelligibly, it is there. Obligation happens before we can possess it, domesticate it, coral it for our own purposes, even just to make it manageable. It is something beyond domestication—an unruly call to affirmation. Affirmation is a belated response to the call, a confirmation of obligation before we are free to choose. The call exposes the passivity of obligation before we are reasonably ready to make a choice, an asymmetry arising from something transcendent, from a time immemorial.

Levinas suggests that the asymmetrical response is an obligation oriented outward, toward the other. He often marks *the other* with words such as the neighbor, the stranger, the widow, the orphan—words used by ancient Hebrew prophets to name the vulnerable in ancient Israelite society. Although on the surface these are empirical terms, identifying actual groups of people in distinction from others, for Levinas they also indicate something structural about responsibility. The 'something that is not me' is structurally experienced as something that is vulnerable, fragile, exposed, in a precarious position. Obligation doesn't just accidentally happen, but it is a structural feature of intersubjective relations. Obligation, a testimony to the normativity of the enigmatic call that originates in a time immemorial, comes via others as vulnerable and exposed. It is felt rather than understood; it cannot be fully grasped although it can clearly be experienced as an affective disruption. The normativity of the call *reveals* us as responsible beings; we *become* responsible subjects through affirmative responses.

The call of normativity thus provides the obligation for living here and now, affecting us in present without being present to mind. Being obedient to the call means the impossibility of abandoning that obligation.

To abandon one's obligation would really be tantamount to abandoning the very structure of one's deepest subjectivity. Despite its enigma, the impossibility of shaping it into a well-formed mental representation, its normativity requires affirming action here and now, before we are in a position to judge whether we ought to say yes. We are obligated to respond affirmatively here in society, and at this time, before we are sure it's safe to affirm, before we are in a position to judge whether rationally it is prudent to do so, prior to knowing exactly what to do.

This is not a responsibility freely chosen, voluntarily shouldered, or the result of rational choice. It is a responsibility that comes before autonomy. My responsibility for the neighbor and stranger is *before* freedom—from a time immemorial. That responsibility concretely comes as call from the vulnerable other. Responsibility is no ordinary call, but a call that disturbs the present in the present without being present, coming in from the outside, from who knows exactly where—before we are ready to domesticate it, an enigma.

As an enigma, it remains safe from our possible memories, brought reasonably to mind. Surely, we must respond consciously and cognitively. To do otherwise would ultimately lead to injustice. We must respond by making reasonable plans to bring about human flourishing wherever and whenever we come face to face with human suffering and pain. This requires that we act deliberately, in our responses to the call, via deliberate social policies and practices. But the enigma of responsibility will keep us from confusing our individual and collective responses with the felt normativity of the call itself. We have some control over the content of our responses, namely, our concrete commitments to alleviating suffering and pain in the world. But we have no control over the call to which such commitment is a response. The call is wild, a wild-card, undomesticated. How much commitment is enough? When will the call be discharged? It is this wildness, this call from the wild, which makes it precisely a *response*. A call to responsibility does not by itself give a clear idea of what to do or to whom one is obligated. As a call from the wild, from a time immemorial that comes from before existence, we can never be quite sure what exactly the call to responsibility amounts to. What exactly does the call require of us? We do not know. That is, we do not have clear and distinct knowledge that is guaranteed to be an adequate answer. Our knowledge falls short—knowledge is too cognitive to be a totally adequate response to the call. There is always a gap between the felt call and the reasoned response. The response is a deliberate, cultural action whereas the call comes from beyond, from a time immemorial. The call constantly reverberates, asking for renewed responses. The multiple, finite responses are always changing, contextualized by concrete social and cultural situations.

Because calling, though powerful in its appeal to obligation, lacks clarity in *what* to do, a hesitation opens up. We hesitate in how to act, in what to do. That hesitation, again a temporal metaphor, is a function of the lag between call and response. This hesitation opens up a space. That room is the time in which we might actually *listen to those who suffer*. The stutter-step between call and response is good news because it gives us the time to actually listen to the needy—the poor, the homeless, the suffering, the outcast, the refugee, the undocumented—before we respond. Not being totally certain about the action required by the call means we cannot just come to those in need without listening. It means that an original passivity is inevitable if we are to be responsible. It means we cannot just say to the vulnerable and marginal: 'we know exactly what it is you need, namely, more fiscal responsibility, or less corrupt government, or an overthrow of your corrupt dictator, or mechanized agriculture, or birth-control programs, or a different religion, or a change in sexual orientation.' It means we cannot just come with a plan without first the passive stutter-step of listening. The felt affective disruption of an enigmatic call that says 'do me no harm' or (more positively) 'do me good' creates a hesitation. This hesitation is not an accident, but a function of the mysterious character of the call associated with a deep subjectivity that emerges from something incoming, from beyond the hinge in time, a time immemorial.

Inspiration

There is another transcendent condition: inspiration. This enigmatic experience of transcendence also has to do with the economic, political, and social life here and now, in the early decades of the twenty-first century. What motivates us to try to change what is wrong, especially in the face of imposing obstacles that impede us? What fills us with the animation that moves us to action? Although the answer is not obvious, there are daily examples of countless people who tirelessly work unselfishly toward realizing a way of life that embodies justice and peace for others in society and around the globe. In this section I argue that this felt affect, this ethical orientation, is the inspiration to hope.

Inspiration is an enigmatic experience of something transcendent. The temporal direction here is futural. Whereas time immemorial indicates something beyond memory, this transcendent condition indicates something beyond foreseeable visions. Metaphorically this future cannot be made present, indicated by the phrase 'a time unforeseeable.' This does not mean the time at the end of history. Rather 'a time unforeseeable' is meant to name something enigmatic in the present, namely, that which cannot be envisioned, let alone brought clearly to mind. The trope 'a time unforeseeable' indicates something for the present without itself being fully present as a foreseeable expectation.

The experience of a time unforeseen is indirect—a trace. As an affective disruption of the present, it is a feeling of hope for what rightly appears hopeless, a felt possibility for rejuvenating a hopelessly flawed world. A feeling of hope means not only that the present situation is not the way it ought to be but also that it *can* be different, renewed and transformed into human flourishing. Something transcendent, from beyond vision, breaks through as a trace: hope about the oppressed and marginalized in society because of their gender, race, class, ethnicity, religion, ability, language, ideology, or sexual orientation. From beyond vision, a trace inspires: the situation is not hopeless, it can, and therefore will, be different.

Hope is an inner affect. It is a felt expectation of possible rupture of the present by something better. Hope is precisely the conviction that present trajectories of historical forces are not tamper proof—a strong disbelief in the ironclad grip of historical forces on the present. Hope is conviction about a possible disruption of the present, at any time. People sometimes use the term hope when talking about expecting favorable changes in present circumstances. 'I hope (expect) that the weather will warm up soon' or 'I hope that my institution will give me a raise soon.' But, according to Levinas, "the expectation of fortunate events is not of itself hope" (Levinas, 2001a, p. 91). That is because such events are rightly interpreted as developments of the continuity of time. The causal structure of the past has embedded in it developmental possibilities that, given its unfolding within time, can become actual, some of which are changes favorable to my (our, their) circumstances. It is often those favorable changes, in continuity with the present, that constitute what we typically refer to when we hope for something. These amount to visions, present mental representations oriented to a foreseeable future. They are foreseeable projections into the future, given the present circumstances. The term hope is not appropriate for those visions precisely because they mark a fundamental continuity from the understood present into the foreseeable future.

Instead, the term *hope* is here reserved for expectations that one cannot rightly foresee. Hope comes precisely when reasonable visions are not an option, when we cannot see clearly the possibility of future favorable events, given present circumstances. Hope is hope precisely when such expectations are unreasonable. Raising the possibility of particularly attractive future states becomes hope when such state seem impossible to achieve, when no rational plan of action, no blueprint, no vision, seems to be able to get us there. It is in that setting that hope is the proper term to use. Hope becomes hope when the situation is desperate, when we have no good reason to expect that particular future to come about, when the present situation seems totally irreparable: when visions fail. Rather than continuity, hope is expecting disruptions to the present's trajectory of leading to the foreseeable future. Hope means being convicted, from outside of those expectations, that the set of causal structures presently determining the world in its march to the foreseeable future will not define it. Hope involves a conviction that the unjust present situation will change despite the present trajectory of social and political forces. Hope is not rational, for it means being inspired by the possibility of change for the better in a rationally determined impossible-to-change situation. Hope is the felt inspiration by an unforeseeable future not continuous with the present. Felt hope comes as an affective disruption from beyond the horizon of our presently situated vision—from a time unforeseeable.

The disruptive trace of hope animates an inner response. It gives rise to a spirited animation toward the possibility of flourishing, where joy and delight shine through life's activities. Hope is a thirst for human flourishing which—given what is known about history, brokenness, oppression, greed, and self-interest in the world—will realistically not exist in the foreseeable future. To be inspired to hope is to be, as John Caputo might put it, animated by a prayer for the annulment of the status quo, despite its perceived persistence and hegemony. But hope is not a prayer for some metaphysical endgame at the end of time. Hope must be for the present. The animation of hope is come quickly, for we cannot wait any longer. We need justice now. The painfulness of pain caused by injustice cannot really be made up by some compensation in the distant future. We see this even in daily examples: when someone is the victim of injustice, some people might be tempted to say, 'the perpetrator will get his just retribution later.' But the aggrieved person often laments 'but that won't compensate for the hurt and pain right now.' Levinas suggests, "retribution in the future does not wipe away the pains of the present" (Levinas, 2001a, p. 93). Justice delayed is injustice. Justice must be enacted in the present for it to be just. Human flourishing must be embodied here and now, alleviating the pain and oppression in the moment that it happens, if it is to actually be human flourishing marked by justice. To hope at all is to hope for repairing the present.

So how does hope as a response to a time unforeseeable concretely show up here and now? The evidence for hope involves interruptions by something incoming from elsewhere, a felt inspiration. Hope enthuses. Something seizes me, from the outside, from a place unseen, which instills a positive spirit deep inside. The inspiration of hope, coming from elsewhere, shows up in a deeply personal manner, as an inner subjective change, an affective disturbance. It is an inner change that reorients my intersubjective relations. Concretely, hope shows up precisely in my relationships to the others around me. It shows up in the subjective conviction that I am necessary for the good of human flourishing to be realized here and now. It shows up in the conviction that—although a person might not be able to explain how such good might come about, or why, or when—I am to be part of bringing about such good. Hope is being convicted that personal contributions toward the good are worthwhile and possible.

To be affected by hope is to be affected with joy and delight. These positive affects are evidence of hope, of being inspired from a time unforeseen. The good of human flourishing is joyful. Although it is difficult to explain how such good might come about, the joy and delight embedded in the efforts of bringing about such good, of working toward change for the better, show evidence of transcendent animation, namely, the real possibilities for human flourishing here and now, despite how things seem. Joy and delight accompany the conviction that one's work toward the good is both possible and worthwhile. To be animated by hope is to be convinced that tackling the seemingly impossible is worthwhile. It is to be convinced of the feeling that some joyful good will be realized here and now. It is to feel not only that I am necessary for its realization, but also that its coming is possible and desirable. It is to feel that, despite the obvious rational foolishness of such conviction, my actions will make a delightful difference in the world, that the world can and will become a place of human flourishing, in part through my own actions.

The inspiration to hope involves a deeper subjectivity, a decentering of the self. Being inspired to hope means uncovering a different sense of being a subject. At one level, being a subject involves being an autonomous, sovereign being, one who is in charge. Here, subjectivity involves a center surrounded by a meaningful stage in which the autonomous person initiates actions, perhaps for personal benefit. The subject as a center enjoys sensory experiences, creates visions, and originates actions—the subjectivity of freedom and autonomy. By contrast, the subjectivity involved in being inspired to hope is decentered. A deeper subjectivity is revealed, one affected by something incoming, convicted by something not of one's own choosing. One's centeredness has been disrupted by something outside of itself.

The affective disruption that comes from a time unforeseen creates a gap. Between the incoming inspiration and the subject's response is a lag, a hesitation. Our hopeful responses are rationally blinkered, for inspiration does not *dictate* to the subject exactly what needs to be done. The gap between hope and action across which the animation of inspiration jumps creates room for an ethical relation. Without a space that reopens again and again, there would be little ethical room for the inspired subject in its relation to the other. Without the stutter of a lag, the subject's own ideas would smother the incoming animation. The gap ruptures the centered action dictated by the foreseeable future, allowing something foreign to emerge in the subject. The non-indifference toward the suffering others keeps domestication from occurring. That breach becomes an opening to listening to those around oneself rather than domesticating the others around one's own purposes.

The notion of a 'time unforeseeable' is meant to protect the enigma of inspiration from misuse. The subject might mistake its rational vision for the future with the transcendent dimension that inspires. In this mistaken identity, hope can be co-opted into a clear picture that is rationally planned, a blueprint for action. This domesticates hope. Such is often the clear-visioned, blueprinted domestication of hope, in which bringing about future perfection becomes a site of current violence because we might see its arrival by means of a blueprint that enacts our own all-too-clear visions. So, to categorize inspiration as coming from a time unforeseeable is to keep it safe from such domestication, from domestic violence.

Avoiding domestication means acknowledging a gap, a delay, a stutter, a hesitation to action. Action originates from within, from the person as an autonomous subject. As such, action involves carrying out internal intent. No hesitation: confidently moving forward, with resolve and commitment. In the autonomy tradition, that is considered the first move. A set of originary, rational principles dictate courses of action and frameworks of rational beliefs supporting such action. But the presence of a stutter-step between inspiration and action opens up a unique opportunity for being touched by the other. That hesitation creates the location for the possibility of being influenced from the outside by those toward whom one is inspired to act. The stutter in the step of action gives pause for being affected by the marginal and victimized. In short, the gap opens up space for the ethical. The other person appears in the gap created by the affective disruption from the time unforeseeable. The other through whom inspiration arrives is, therefore, not straightforwardly present, in the subject's own presence, as a figure known and represented in consciousness without remainder—a figure known because it has been grasped or comprehended by cognition. No, the other person's relation to the subject—in his or her vulnerability and marginalization—is safe from such domestication. The inspired subject cannot avoid the incoming animation. Such animation creates a non-indifference in the subject—this is what Levinas means when he says that the subject's relation to the other is its relation to the future. The ethical character of hope is that it is for the other, the other's flourishing, not one's own. What makes it an ethical hope is that it is a hope for others, for their welfare, for their flourishing, for their well-being. Here and now. In Iran and Afghanistan, Congo and Syria, the South Bronx and Southern Mexico.

2
Learning

Abstract: *This chapter develops a deeper understanding of the student and learning. By recasting the student's subjectivity in terms of a deep relation to the teacher as other, it suggest that the learning process involves welcoming an external disturbance, something the chapter develops as the inspirational nature of what Levinas calls the ethical. This situates and relativizes the traditional model of the student as autonomous self-learner. The Levinasian notion involves interpreting human subjectivity radically as intersubjective, in terms of inspiration, which comes through the teacher.*

Keywords: autonomy; hope; inspiration; learner; learning; Levinas

Joldersma, Clarence W. *A Levinasian Ethics for Education's Commonplaces: Between Calling and Inspiration.* New York: Palgrave Macmillan, 2014. DOI: 10.1057/9781137415493.0006.

In this chapter I re-situate the student and what we typically call learning. I will describe the subjectivity of the student in terms of his or her relation to the teacher *as other*. By this I mean that being a learner, at its deepest, is being someone who welcomes an external disturbance, an inspiration that is ethical. Learning involves a deep subjectivity, one oriented by a felt affect called inspiration, something that comes *through* the teacher. This situates the traditional model of the subjectivity of the student as self-learner.

Learning conditioned by inspiration is marked by the enigmatic experience of hope. This is the ethical current that ought to orient this commonplace of formal schooling—the ethical relation that conditions learning points to something transcendent in the learning event. This requires us to unsettle a dominant view of the learner and learning by using the idea of deeper subjectivity developed in the previous chapter. I will suggest that below our usual understanding of the learner is a subjectivity that ethically orients learning from another. This makes explicit that learning is conditioned by what I have called transcendence. The transcendent condition that gives learning its ethical orientation, the relation to the teacher as other, also orients learning outward to the world, via the call of justice.

Of course, there actually is no single, generic description of *the* student. All flesh-and-blood students come to schools as members of multiple groupings—gender, class, race, ability, personality, language, ethnicity, religion, sexual orientation. These memberships are inevitable, thus also crucial, for understanding their success in learning something, and more specifically, being taught by someone. Although most of the time teachers might behave as if there is such a being as *the* student abstracted from all the concrete particulars of embodiment, social groupings and personal biography, in reality this is at best a convenient, organizational fiction. Furthermore, actual students have varying degrees of success in a variety of specific ways, something that requires careful empirical investigation by the social sciences of the discipline of education.

However, my study is not an empirical investigation. And there is legitimacy in discussing *the* student abstractly. Mine is a high-altitude analysis, where the more empirically specific factors remain implicit. I focus on the conditions that constitute learning's ethical orientation. Although my discussion explores the conditions that might help us interpret what happens when a student is actually taught by someone, it is not meant to be a prescription for effective learning or tips for how to avoid ineffective studying. That is, my discussion is not a piece of psychologically or sociologically framed empirical educational research. Instead, it is a philosophical discussion of the ethical conditions that frame being taught by another. In developing these ideas, I rely on the ideas developed in the previous chapter. My focus on transcendent conditions gives a better understanding of the ethical orientation that grounds a learner's relation when being taught by another, a teacher.

The student as autonomous

A traditional way to characterize the subjectivity of students is by using the idea of autonomy. Characterizing the student as someone who gains knowledge is often aligned in our social imaginary with a concept of self-development. More broadly, student autonomy is often a stated goal of school learning.

In this approach, formal schooling interprets the nature of being a student by telling a story of developing autonomy, where autonomy means being self-directed and controlled. This was not only the message of Locke, Rousseau, and Kant, but recent educational theorists have also advocated this understanding of the student. For example, Meira Levinson argues that formal education is obligated "to help [students] develop their capacities for autonomy" (Levinson, 1999, p. 7). This is often interpreted as freeing the mind from its domination by emotions and the senses, by culture and society. In this model, the learner is understood as a subject who can purify his or her mind of emotions, opinion, belief, cultural prejudices, and so forth by acquiring a passion for reason (Joldersma, 2011b). To be a learner is to become a rational master over what has been restrictive; to be a learner is to become autonomous.

Much of the autonomy discussion comes from a third-person perspective. A neutral observer, neither the teacher nor the student, describes the student in these terms. This is not a description from the student's perspective, but a third-person description of a socially approved, externally imposed desired effect in the student. I would like to shift the perspective, to the first-person perspective of the student to address the question of autonomy and being a learner. From a first-person perspective it isn't clear that my goal as a student is to develop autonomy. I might well be perfectly content in my non-autonomous state. I may be smugly satisfied with reveling in my instincts, cheering loudly for the irrational partisanship within which I was raised, and living with reckless abandon according to the natural desires that well up within. More likely I am in school to learn some chemistry and writing, to earn a high school diploma or college degree, recognizing that I can't do this on my own, and thus need a teacher, if only as external verification that I put in the requisite seat time (Labaree, 2010). From my perspective as a student, it isn't clear that I'm consciously developing autonomy, although perhaps the cunning of reason will prevail and it will develop in me behind my back.

Central to autonomy is that one has deliberate, conscious control over one's beliefs and desires. In the enlightenment tradition, this means putting one's motives as well as one's actions before the tribunal of one's own rational will (Kant, 1996). Thus my experience of my own (developing) autonomy is the conscious, deliberate control I develop over non-rational beliefs and desires. Intrinsic to the autonomy model is consciousness; it is the *conscious* subject that develops rational autonomy, and learning is geared to developing such autonomy. This involves deliberately representing one's natural desires to oneself, including their connections to possible long-term negative consequences if followed unchecked. It involves comparing one's projected wishes with more reasonably envisioned outcomes. And it involves representing to oneself the beliefs that one has unreflectively held to be true—about, say, members of another race or ethnicity, and examining them for inconsistencies, flaws, and irrational foundations—and holding them up against the reality of actual members of such a race or ethnicity.

There is much to admire in this. Autonomy should play an important role in the maturing process, and it clearly doesn't always develop by default. Moreover, in the face of a sea of advertising that appeals to the emotions and basic instincts, and in the reality of wave after wave of irrational and fear-charged political partisanship, to have some reasonable mastery over these elements that might otherwise control the subject is a very good thing. Formal schooling that attempts to foster autonomy is laudable. Good schooling requires endeavoring to develop autonomy in students.

Autonomy is not only about first-person control over emotions and desires, but also centrally includes gaining knowledge of the world. Learning about the world involves a model of consciousness. Philosophical models of consciousness typically take as central the notion of intentionality, the idea of "consciousness of" or aboutness. Intentionality is a relation between a subject and something outside the subject, where consciousness involves an object presented to consciousness. On this understanding, subjects can be thought as learning about something when they direct their attention to, thereby coming to know, this or that. Or, perhaps more accurately, coming to know this *as* that; to learn is to correlate *this* thing in with *that* idea. Learning is finding connections between thing and idea or being and concept, bringing a conception to bear on something strange, using *that* idea to disclose *this* being. Learning on this construal centrally involves consciousness—the intentionality that correlates thought and object.

In doing so, the object is *determined* by the learning subject. The object is construed as constituted by consciousness through endowing it with meaning through reference. Intentionality's arrow involves meaning-giving by capturing the multiplicity of what is given to consciousness through thematizing them as realities stable enough to be identified. As an act of synthesis, thematization picks out the important and enduring, clear constants in the plenitude of sensibility that is given. Constructivism, for example, has this construal of learning (Joldersma, 2011a).

In this understanding, learning is understood to involve the freedom of the subject through overcoming the world's resistance. The conscious subject encompasses its exteriority in revealing the world as known. Making the strange familiar simultaneously secures the subject from alienation. The world's resistance to thought disappears through cognitive mastery. Intentionality's arrow, secured at one end, is deployed in acts of centering by the conscious subject: learning constitutes acts of freedom. Learning is not only representing the world but, more strongly, constituting it through representation. The learner as conscious subject brings the world to presence, in the present, working from the inside out. This is central to autonomy. Whereas sometimes autonomy is construed as the *goal* for learning, actually the learner *is* an autonomous subject. The conscious subject is the center-point of power, able to deliberately represent, constituting the meanings and references of such mental representations. Autonomy is not merely the goal of learning but is embedded in its very structure. Learning, on this construal, is portrayed as self-directed, originating from within.

The model of the conscious subject as autonomous in learning does not adequately explain the ethical relation involved in learning from another. Depicting learning as comprehending the world through constituting is not only a strength, but also a weakness. This model has difficulty showing how one is open to influences from a teacher or why that influence is ethical precisely because it depicts learning as self-learning, initiated from within. The conscious subject is a centered ego, an "I," in which knowledge of the world is actively gathered or constructed (Joldersma, 2011a). Although in this model, a conscious subject is construed as able to learn about the world by itself, its very independence makes it difficult to explain how it is possible, let alone ethical, to be taught by a teacher.

Yet learning from another is a ubiquitous, if not necessary, phenomenon. More strongly, we learn from a teacher because we are in no position to learn by ourselves. Learning happens precisely before we have an inadequate conceptual matrix. It requires relinquishing inadequate conceptualizations or erroneous assumptions before one really knows what is more adequate. Becoming critical of oneself requires an *other*, a teacher, from whom one learns to be self-critical. Of course, if it is to lead to autonomy, learning from another cannot simply be a purely passive reception of information transferred from the teacher to the student. Those championing the autonomy of the student are quite right about criticizing simple information transfer as an inadequate model. It not only undermines the learning typically associated with becoming autonomous, but it also does not adequately depict the intersubjective relation between teacher and student.

The inadequacy of the autonomy model is not the same as its total failure. Instead, it suggests that the model cannot stand alone in explaining how one learns from another. Although there is much to be said for the intentionality of the "consciousness of" model, it requires complication. I will do so by uncovering a hidden subjectivity, one that conditions consciousness. I will suggest that learning from a teacher is conditioned by an intersubjective relationship that is deeper than consciousness. What I am questioning is the *founding* role of consciousness for learning from another. Instead, I will give a more primary role to corporeality by drawing on Levinas's concept of inspiration. It will reveal a deeper subjectivity in the relation of learning from another. This subjectivity does not negate the subject-as-consciousness, but connects learning to a more original subjectivity. My goal is not to replace the subjectivity we call autonomy, but to reveal a deeper one. That subjectivity constitutes the ethical orientation that animates learning.

The inspired subject

In situating the autonomy model, I will argue that the character of human subjectivity at its deepest is something other than consciously developed autonomy. The first-person autonomy of the learner is situated in a first-person heteronomous subjectivity, one that I call the inspired subject. Levinas's idea of the heteronomous subject is intrinsically connected to the idea of radical intersubjectivity, also the topic of the next section. In this section I'm after understanding intersubjectivity as the transcendent condition for learning to set up the argument that ethical inspiration orients learning, including what we characterized above as developing autonomy. In doing so, I will be building on what in Chapter 2 I depicted as transcendence. Inspiration is, from a first-person perspective, an enigmatic experience that seeps into consciousness. It comes in from elsewhere but shows itself as deeply personal.

Beneath the freedom associated with autonomy is subjectivity that exhibits dependency and openness. To be a bodily subject is to depend on the very earth from which one arose, and thus also to be vulnerable to decay and demise. The success of life's struggle is always momentary, accompanied by worry and anxiety about tomorrow. The affect of worry arises in feeling that one's joy might well be fleeting, labile, momentary, and prone to disappear. It is because of this affect that our freedom turns into the agency of self-preservation, for the worry about tomorrow becomes concern for self-protection today. The conscious, autonomous subject's worry conditions the practical activities of tool-making, shelter-building, and food-growing. These everyday actions are grounded in the worry for tomorrow, about the possible demise of the independent self. And although not as obvious, the worry for tomorrow also grounds activities such as accumulating money, organizing societies, and developing knowledge for power—these too are manifestations of the very primal worry for self-preservation. The worrying subject is the human being of everyday life: shopping, working, eating, going to movies, traveling, hating, getting angry, sleeping, complaining about the government, and enjoying the sunshine on the beach.

The conscious subject's activities conditioned by worry are a function of its permanent dependence. The subject worries it cannot survive without living in a dwelling, without property to sustain it. A dwelling is a place of safety into which the subject can bring possessions. And possessions are not property without a secure place to have control over them. The subject on this view can be thought of as the one who possesses. The subject is a centered being, but one who actively maintains that independence by accumulating and controlling property within the sphere of one's dwelling. The world is construed as potential support for, or possible threat to, one's home life. This freedom has long been associated with the autonomous subject. Knowledge on this view is one such central possession—a kind of property we control. The words we often use to describe knowledge suggest this: we grasp an idea, retain information, and comprehend a concept. This is the language of control and mastery connected to autonomy. These metaphors speak of possessing knowledge, creating space in the world for oneself, actively bringing knowledge into our home as property, masterfully keeping one's beliefs under control.

Levinas suggests that this is not a good place to stop. Or, more accurately, it is not the right place to start. Although he does not deny this notion of subjectivity, and doesn't *replace* it with something else, he argues that it isn't the rock-bottom idea of what it means to be a subject. He often quotes Pascal, which is still very germane in our times: all wars start with someone saying, "this is my place in the sun" (Levinas, 1998b, p. 130). The source of all violence, suggests Levinas, is precisely the spontaneous concern for self-preservation, seeking and maintaining one's place in the sun, challenging others who might wish to usurp that place. The self-preserving subject striving for its independence is prone to violence and evil. To relativize this, Levinas uncovers a deeper subjectivity, one that he portrays in a variety of ways. Here I will do so in terms of *inspiration* (Joldersma, 2008). In the previous chapter we depicted the notion of inspiration as being susceptible to something incoming, something that gives rise to a feeling of hope. What I did not develop was the concrete avenue through which this experience arises. Subjectivity as primordial susceptibility implies being susceptible to something. Inspiration suggests that a radical intersubjectivity lies at the heart of subjectivity. Here I will develop further the radical character of this intersubjectivity as something that shows up in the relation to the other as transcendent, as one who can and does invade the ego, as an unbidden disturbance.

This idea of subjectivity is quite different from the more traditional one of autonomy and freedom, parsed out above in terms of self-preservation and property accumulation. As stated before, Levinas is not seeking to *replace* the notion of the autonomous subject, but is suggesting that autonomy isn't the deepest core of what it means to be a subject. This is important for Levinas because he thinks that the violence of protecting one's place in the sun comes precisely when autonomy and freedom are taken to be the deepest defining moments of subjectivity. What Levinas seeks is something deeper, a notion of the subject that will contextualize and relativize the subject as autonomous.

Inspiration is centrally associated with bodiliness, and in particular its standing openness and exposure to something incoming. To be inspired is to be affected by something from the outside, and to respond to that disturbance in an animated manner. In general, inspiration shows itself in the bodily responses of non-indifference to the other. The subject's standing exposure is for Levinas a deeper notion of subjectivity, where the subject's independence is relativized by its dependence. Being a subject involves the openness to something incoming, a vulnerability and exposure to something external. The dominant reaction of the subject to this has been to protect and defend, to assert sovereignty and freedom. Levinas is suggesting that our vulnerability exposes a deeper subjectivity, one that comes before or beyond its independence and autonomy. The core of this vulnerability lies in an inescapable intersubjectivity. It signals an inescapable relation to the other person, something he most often simply calls the other.

For Levinas, the category of *the other* is crucial for a deeper understanding of the subject and subjectivity (Levinas, 1987, p. 39). The idea of the other is the other person outside of our expectations and conceptualizations, outside of the subject's autonomy and freedom, outside of its worry or concern for self-preservation, before it makes judgments about the other's identity, abilities, dangerousness, attractiveness, and utility. These characteristics, important and real as they are, come afterward, as part of the subject's self-preservation mode, defending 'my place in the sun,' that is, its autonomy. The idea of the other indicates the other person beyond the subject's freedom.

Inspiration literally means, in its physiological sense, taking air into the body, that is, breathing in. Levinas uses the notion of inspiration to indicate that the other creates a fission in the unity of the centered subject. Inspiration undoes the independent nature of the autonomous subject by breaking up the naiveté of its centeredness. The autonomous subject is a self-satisfied unity, whereas the inspired subject is disturbed, its identity divided. The other enters the very interior of the subject as something foreign, undermining the subject's feeling of self-sufficiency. Below the self-sufficient *I*, inspiration reveals a responding *me*.

Inspiration is an ethical animation. Levinas says, "In responsibility for the other we are at the heart of the ambiguity of inspiration" (Levinas, 1998d, p. 149). The ethical is a relation to the other that uncovers the heteronomous depth of the ego's subjectivity. Inspiration, as an ethical relation to the other, coming in as an interruption of freedom and sovereignty, reveals the ego's deeper subjectivity. Inspiration disturbs its preoccupation with self-preservation and questions the naiveté of its centeredness. Inspiration seeps into the subject's conscious autonomy, upsetting its sovereign agency. More generally, inspiration by the other puts into question the primacy of the idea of the subject defined as autonomous. The interrupted, questioned subject is what comes to light in the relation to the other, uncovering a subjectivity that is more original than that of freedom. It exposes a decentered subject, showing it to be grounded in radical, originary intersubjectivity. In short, it makes explicit the heteronomy that conditions the autonomous subject.

Although the term heteronomous can mean several things, I employ it to indicate a subject defined not first as free but in terms of inspiration. This sense of subject is more primary than that of freedom. The depth of subjectivity is an ethical relationship to the other; this primordial subjectivity is hidden when we model subjectivity exclusively as agency and autonomy. The relationship with the other uncovers the subjectivity of being inspired by the other.

The asymmetry of learning

We can now depict the ethical relation associated with learning. Describing the subjectivity of the student in terms of inspiration makes visible the ethical orientation that animates learning. Central to that ethical connection is the asymmetry of the relationship of the student to the teacher. From the depth of an inspired subject the teacher functions as the *other*. As inspired, the student is in a heteronomous relationship with the teacher, showing something transcendent that disrupts the learner as an autonomous subject, decentering it by inspiring the student not to cling to his or her own conscious centeredness. From this depth perspective, the teacher is outside student's autonomy and freedom precisely in the teaching function. Teaching for the inspired student situates the teacher in the position of the other, outside the student's conscious conceptualization, understanding, prejudices, assumptions, beliefs. The inspiration that grounds learning involves having the teacher outside of the learner's consciousness.

Heteronomy sets up the possibility of the student's understanding—preconceptions, beliefs, knowledge, attitudes, values, motivations—being called into question. For a student, the grounds for learning something from a teacher come through an opening created by the rupture of the student's current coherence and totality of understanding. The possibility for learning something from someone requires an interruption of a certain complacency and naiveté that are naturally part of being human. The centered subject is egoistic. Its concern is for itself, and understands the world as surroundings with itself at the center. The egoism of the centered subject shows up in the joy of independence and freedom and in the worry about maintaining or preserving one's self against the world and others in the world. The opening for learning from a teacher comes precisely because the teacher as other interrupts, disrupts, disturbs, ruptures such coherence and equilibrium, something that comes from outside the coherence and stability. The condition for learning involves having one's autonomy problematized, one's freedom put into question, exactly for the sake of learning. To be a student at a deep level is to be in a heteronomous relationship with the teacher, as other.

This disruption is the felt affect of inspiration. The condition for learning is being inspired. This is openness to the teacher as one who questions, openness to interruptions to the student's egoism, including self-preservation. The teacher is felt as a foreign disturbance entering into the interiority of the student as a subject, undermining its self-sufficiency and naïve self-satisfaction. Inspiration is felt as the autonomous *I* of the student becoming answerable to the teacher as other, feeling assigned to respond. The independent *I* of the student is conditioned by the inspired *I*. It means feeling disturbed by something that did not originate from within, but came from elsewhere. It means feeling an *in*-fluence of something that comes from outside of the student's world—outside of the learner's conceptualization, grasp, control, expectation, and manipulation.

This idea can be stated with the metaphor of a time unforeseen in order to depict the enigmatic character of this condition for learning. Learning from another occurs in situations in which the learner cannot foresee. To be able to foresee means to be able to absorb what is incoming, to assimilate it into the subject's current conceptual structures and thought patterns, without significant change. It is to be able to expect what is incoming, to anticipate it. But that is precisely the opposite of being disturbed, having one's autonomy questioned. The ability to absorb without changing is, in fact, to be autonomous, in charge, independent, complacent. Inspiration, by contrast, is experiencing something unforeseen. Learning occurs in response to being disturbed precisely because the interruption cannot be anticipated, because it is unexpected. Learning from another occurs in a space of blindness, beyond vision, that seeps into consciousness as a presence and absence. Learning from another is conditioned not by the joy of independence or the spontaneity of freedom and agency, but instead by inspiration from the other which functions as a disturbance from a time unforeseen that cannot be fully recovered into presence.

But there's more than just being disturbed, put into question, beyond expectation. It is a disturbance with an ethical orientation. If this questioning is coerced, done against one's wishes, without permission, it might rightly be called violence. Violence threatens, obliterates, destroys. But learning—as learning—builds up, constructs, enhances. So this disturbance, in order to be an opening for learning, is not violent, but something ethical. Learning, although unforeseen, is a disturbance welcomed by the student. The student as learner must welcome the impossible, feel hope in the disturbance. To use the metaphor of dwelling, learning involves an opening of hospitality. To be a learner is to be hospitable, to invite the teacher as other into one's dwelling, to ask the teacher to make him or herself comfortable, at home. Learning requires being a gracious host, welcoming the incoming disturbance. The door is open—the walls are not battered down from the outside. The teacher, as other, is *invited* in for learning. It is the welcome that most clearly signals inspiration as an ethical orientation, an infusion of hope, a hope for rejuvenation beyond the disturbance, for something better.

This means that having a dwelling is important for learning's ethical orientation. Without a home, there could be no invitation, no welcoming, no hospitality. That is, without the enjoying and worrying dimensions of the subject, one who has both enjoyment and concern for self in terms of preservation, there could be no welcoming the questioning of that freedom and enjoyment, namely, one's autonomy. The ethical orientation of learning thus requires the at-home nature of autonomy. Its disturbance via inspiration does not abolish the autonomous subject, but interrupts its complacency and serenity. Although the condition for learning is inspiration, it requires something to be inspired, a subjectivity that dwells in a home.

The learning relation I am describing has a distinct asymmetry. The asymmetry shows up in the disturbance, the unexpectedness, and the welcoming. Disturbances are not symmetrical, for they are only such from the perspective of the one disturbed. Similarly, to get something not expected is only such from the recipient's point of view. And welcoming can only be done by the one whose place it is. The asymmetry that conditions the student's relation to the teacher is not half a reciprocal relation. The conditions for being a learner are not simultaneously those that condition being a teacher; the teacher, from the student's perspective, is the one who is welcomed, the one who delivers something unexpected. Only the learner welcomes the one who disturbs, who brings something unexpected. What this highlights is that being a learner involves an asymmetry from a first-person perspective. More strongly, the core of the ethical relation of learning is its asymmetric relationship, one that has no reciprocity as such. The phrase 'the inspired subject' is meant to indicate that ethical asymmetry.

Of course, any particular flesh-and-blood person may indeed function at times as teacher and at other times as learner. People who are employed as professors can and do learn many things from the school's tuition payers. Or, high school teachers who are paid to teach can and do, in fact, learn from their teenage students. But in those cases, to the extent professors and high school teachers are learning, at the very moment they function as learners, they are inspired by their students, and thus are conditioned by a relation of asymmetry with the other from whom they are at that moment learning. That is, professional instructors are at that moment inspired subjects, existing in an asymmetric intersubjective relation with their students, who function in that relation as the disturbing, questioning, other.

Inspiration for learning

I have been arguing that although consciousness is undoubtedly involved in the process of learning, it is inspiration that gives learning its ethical orientation. I would like to approach this briefly from the angle of what Levinas calls hypostasis, something I develop more fully in the next chapter. Hypostasis is the continual renewal of one's interiority, an achievement that involves living from what is outside oneself. Hypostasis means that one's existence is always evanescent, that its continual emergence simultaneously involves fading away into the unknown desert of bare existence. Hypostasis is a helpful concept to illuminate how learning is necessary and how it might be described. The learning subject must constantly renew itself by bringing into itself not only food and oxygen, but also information, conceptualizations, and understandings. Learning is part of the subject's more general renewal efforts of hypostasis.

The phenomenon of enjoyment is central to this renewal. Actively assimilating elements from the outside is part of the love of life. This involves more than merely physical or biological elements, for the incoming cognitive elements also are assimilated with the same love of life. The assimilatory character of learning and cognition is grounded in enjoyment. Although we tend to focus on the utility of what is being learned—skills, knowledge, facts, and dispositions—the very act of assimilation constituting learning is part of being an enjoying subject. It is part of the more general hypostatic subject living from the elements, aside from worrying about whether it is enough or the right material, from how well the cognitive material has been mastered or whether it will be useful in the future. At a level more basic than utility, the acts of assimilation by the learning subject are done in enjoyment, precisely because the learner is, at a very deep level, an enjoying subject. Enjoyment is a spontaneous and internally generated affect involved in learning. Such spontaneity marks a kind of freedom, the sheltering freedom of an interior organization not determined purely by exterior forces.

But enjoyment also implies vulnerability. Because enjoyment requires assimilation of elements from the outside, it simultaneously means a continuing openness to outside disturbances. This adds something to the phenomenon of learning. Rather than 'merely' assimilating, learning simultaneously involves exposure to interruption. Disturbances might well lead to unwelcome rupture of oneself as a subject, including one's very identity. To learn is to be influenced, something that requires being vulnerable. The learner, situated in the love of life, is simultaneously exposed to interruptions of that life. On the one hand the learning event centers and separates the enjoying subject from the exterior forces while on the other it undermines that centeredness and independence. Learning is situated at that dynamic tension, involving at once the centeredness and independence of the joy of assimilation *and* the vulnerability of being disturbed, disrupted, and ruptured. The standing possibility of interruption and rupture is a normal and necessary counterpart for the possibility of learning from another person, a teacher. Learning is not only a move toward autonomy and independence, but it also necessarily continues to involve a standing heteronomy and dependence.

An ethical orientation is important because learning is not merely an act of wonderment and assimilation but involves a self-critical position—the possibility of being undone. This is not first a self-conscious let alone cognitive act, but rather one that is generated from the outside although felt as deeply personal. It is an orientation toward one's existing knowledge and understanding, one of welcoming outside elements that call into question one's existing network of information and perspectives, one's cherished assumptions and preconceptions. Asking questions of oneself doesn't happen by itself, but involves something coming in from the outside, an outside disturbance that unsettles the interiority of the centered subject. A stance of questioning is conditioned by an ethical orientation to the interrupting teacher, as other. The critical mode is first an ethically oriented affect precipitated by something that one is not yet in a position to judge for its appropriateness. The disturbance is an inspiration from the teacher that makes possible a self-critical stance.

A self-critical stance is really the inescapability of interior change through learning. As stated previously, learning is grounded in the hypostatic character of openness. One way to characterize that openness in the context of learning is through listening. We might think of listening as an act of reception, that of receiving (orally) information, ideas, and so forth. But listening also involves a more profound passivity—a radical openness to what is other. In learning, the receptivity to new information or novel understandings involves this deeper passivity. This is a standing exposure that is deeper than the act of receptive assimilation. The deeper passivity of listening is the risk of being open to the teacher as other, outside of one's existing expectations and assumptions, existing knowledge and frameworks. Listening as radical passivity is an exposure to the possibility of being undone, before one is in a cognitive position to judge about the appropriateness of the content of what is incoming. Listening is the risk of being influenced by the teacher before one is ready for it.

Listening is central to one's deep subjectivity. At one level, the hypostatic subject as an interior space is a place of protection from the exterior, a shelter or dwelling. But listening signals a standing openness of the hypostatic subject, unsettling such protection. Listening is the inability to not be disturbed by the influence of the teacher as other; this gives the incoming disturbance access to the interiority of the learner. Listening is welcoming the disturbance, making it an ethical relation to the other. Listening is a form of hospitality, an invitation that gives its passivity an ethical orientation. Listening is an ethical relationship.

Learning involves responding. Listening is not yet the complete act of learning by itself. That response I will call speaking. Now, typically we identify speaking with someone conveying some content or meaning to another person. However I want to distinguish between the content of what is said and the activity of speaking itself. What I'm interested in is the gesture of speaking, bracketing the content. This is what Levinas calls *saying*: "Saying is communication, to be sure, but as a condition for all communication, as exposure" (Levinas, 1998d, p. 48). The response I'm calling speaking (saying) is first a risk, a vulnerability. As a response to listening, it again opens the learning subject to exposure, although in a different way than before. It exposes the learner's unsettled and newly reconstituted interiority to the other. Speaking as saying thus marks, once again, the heteronomy of the learner in relation to the teacher as other. In speaking to a teacher, that is, by answering a question or venturing an idea to a prompt, undertaking a project, the student is responding. As a response it asks for acknowledgment by the teacher as other. Speaking as saying is a sign that asks the teacher as other to affirm its adequacy. As a sign to the teacher the response shows the primordial inspiration of the student to the teacher as other, revealing a continuing asymmetry in relation to the teacher. In being *inspired* by the teacher, the relationship shows an ethical orientation.

Both listening and speaking are asymmetrical relations between the learner and the other. Levinas says, "Conversation...maintains the distance between me and the other ..." (Levinas, 1969, p. 40). From the perspective of the listening and speaking learner, there is a continuing distance in the relationship with the teacher as other. Conversation occurs across the gap of difference between oneself and the other. Communication does not erase that gap, but needs that gap for it to occur. Rather than fusing the difference or closing the gap, speaking as saying requires the student's ongoing inability to be non-indifferent to the teacher. That is, the student is inspired by the teacher as other.

This structure situates the learner as autonomous subject, including its cognitive intentionality. Autonomy—the centeredness of agency, including the cognitive and conscious agency of forming intentional representations—is situated in the listening and speaking subject. Speaking and listening are relations that condition developing objects of cognitive intentionality—the content of speech, what is *said*. The primordial relations of speaking and listening are prior to this, involving the other to whom I am offering something. Although what is said is a function of cognitive intentionality, and thus autonomy, it can take place only by being grounded in my offering this to the other.

Speaking as saying reinforces the idea that learning is ethically oriented in its being conditioned by something transcendent. Although learning as a cognitive act involves a centering activity, namely the intentional arrow of thematization, speaking as saying conditions consciousness. Saying is a function of a relation with the other that is felt as an ethical claim by the other. The condition for cognitive content is the standing possibility of being judged as being incorrect in what is said. At its deepest, then, the process of learning involves "the risky uncovering of oneself, in sincerity, the breaking up of inwardness, and the abandon of all shelter, exposure to traumas, vulnerability" (Levinas, 1998d, p. 48). Learning in its depth is a fine risk. What is said is conditioned by the release of that content from the shelter of one's interiority. For learning to occur, cognitive intentionality—the outward directed arrow of cognitive content to the object of cognition—is offered to someone else for affirmation, and the risk of being wrong. Learning thus cannot merely be an interior process as a function of autonomy, as if learning is merely always self-formation. Rather, learning occurs in the ethical space of non-indifference constituted by the ethical relation of inspiration by the teacher as other. This is the space of welcoming the teacher's judgment, which means that the learner is a decentered subject. The condition for new cognitive formation in the learner's interiority is the welcome disturbance constituted by the offering of what is said to the teacher as other. By *saying* this to the other, the cognitive content has as its permanent underlying ground an ethical orientation to the other.

My argument has been that learning is at its deepest a relational phenomenon—an ethical relation between oneself as a learner and the teacher as other. If the process of knowing remains the core of what constitutes learning, then we must see this as grounded in the relations of speaking and listening, that is, in the ethical relations of inspiration by the other.

In the first chapter I stated that education's transcendent conditions concretely manifest itself in call and inspiration. Education, on the one hand, is conditioned by normative obligation and, on the other, by motivating hope. Learning from another is an exercise in hope. Learning something new is, in a very real sense for the learner, cognitively impossible. That is, under a certain description either it is something within the learner's conceptual grasp, and then it is something the learner already knows but perhaps didn't realize, or it is something outside of the learner's grasp, and then it is something the learner really did not know at all, even to the point of not knowing where to turn to obtain it. So, conceptually, learning something new is impossible. But we all know that learning *is* possible. More specifically, we all know learning from another person happens all the time. Schools bank on this rather mundane fact and students pay much tuition for this. So, we have to conclude in a slightly contradictory fashion: something conditions learning to make possible what is impossible.

The experience of inspiration points to this condition. More specifically, learning from another becomes possible because a learner is inspired by the other. Concretely, such inspiration creates hope in the learner. It creates the expectation that, despite present ignorance, something new will be gained, before the student knows exactly what that might be. To be a student is to look forward to the impossible. By 'impossible' I mean something that cannot be foreseen from within, from within the interiority of the subject. It must come from outside, as a disturbance of that interiority. The felt affect of hope is generated by an incoming inspiration, an interruption that is welcomed. Hope is the welcome of an unforeseen disturbance within the learner's interiority.

This points to the transcendent dimension I named a 'time unforeseen,' namely the disruption of the present by something genuinely different, new, better. Inspiration in learning functions as such a disruption for the learner from the perspective of that learner. This makes learning from another possible. Inspiration is evidence of the transcendent dimension, a particular example of how it conditions everyday life, in this case, learning. Learning is conditioned by hope, something unforeseen that one, nevertheless, expects. This makes the inspiration associated with learning a common, everyday manifestation of hope. Hope is our embodied response to inspiration. In particular, hope shows up in the learner's motivation to act in response to the teacher. That otherness of the teacher shows up as something unforeseen by the student, infiltrating as an inspiration. Only because the subject is inspired by the other is it possible to do the impossible, namely, learn something unforeseen by the self. Learning is overcoming the limitations of the student's present knowledge through being inspired by the teacher as other.

The call to responsibility animating justice

Inspiration is not the only transcendent condition for learning. As I noted in Chapter 1, through our response of struggling for justice we experience an ethical *call* that comes from the world. This is the call to live justly and for justice, seeking peace and living peacefully, desiring delight and living delightfully. More particularly, the call for justice comes as an inclusive obligation to help the stranger. Struggling for justice as a real possibility means being animated by hope *and* being called to responsibility to act in moving toward inclusive communities that are marked by human flourishing.

This call has something specific to do with learning. The larger context of a student's inspiration for learning is the call to responsibility for concrete action in the world. This call, coming from beyond the teacher, is an obligation that orients the student outward, beyond the school walls and away from his or her own autonomy and self-interest. The call to struggle for justice comes to the students via what Levinas names the third party or the "other others" (Levinas, 1969, p. 212). Given that the teacher is the immediate other for the learner, for the student there are others who are not the teacher, who also function as other in Levinas's sense. Although formally *all* other people function as other others, concretely the other others most visible are those on the margins in our society and around the globe. If the teacher is the face-to-face other for the student, the vulnerable in society are the other others for that student. This means that the student's obligations are, in the long run, not ultimately to the teacher but to the others.

The other others—especially those on the margins—disturb, question, and disrupt the students' enjoyment and freedom. Those disturbances are not first conceptual but social. The call that comes through the other others interrupts the serenity of the purely cognitive character of the learning process by intruding with the need for social justice, that is, through the responsibility to the vulnerable in society for their human flourishing. The interruptions that condition learning aren't merely formal inspirations of the learners' cognitive apparatus, but more profoundly ethical disturbances of cognitive lives that may otherwise be preoccupied with pure understanding, abstracted from any immediacy. Obligations coming from the world are social responsibilities. It is in its worldly situatedness that this call to the learner manifests itself—the pure cognitive mind is an abstraction from that concrete self. This more substantive understanding of the social call to action gives normative direction to what otherwise might remain a purely cognitive disturbance of the student. Learning obligated by a call directs the learners' understandings to seeing their place in the world as agentive beings working for human flourishing.

In this way, inspiration is connected to call. A call comes through the other others, those on the margins of society and around the globe, to the learner. The call to responsibility from the world reverberates inside the classroom, making it ethically impossible to abandon society. It calls the student to an obligation outside of his or her own self-interest, outside the acquisition of pure disciplinary knowledge. That call obligates the student, as learner, in the direction of the neighbor and the stranger. This call isn't one of the many well-formed mental representations that constitute the knowledge a student may be acquiring at the conscious, cognitive level. Instead, this call comes from beyond such representations, from a time immemorial, as a trace in the present. The student's concrete responsibility ultimately is to the vulnerability of the other others. Evidence of his or her humanity involves being responsible for others. To be a learner, ethically, includes the condition of being a human that is responsible for the suffering in the world. Learning itself, albeit animated through the teacher, is also conditioned by responsibility for the other others.

This is not a responsibility freely chosen, a result of voluntary commitment, but is something that comes as a call through the face of the suffering and the poor. The student's studies are ultimately contextualized as a response to that call. As such, students who gain skills and general knowledge are called to use them to bring about human flourishing wherever and whenever they come face to face with human suffering and pain. Because this call to responsibility comes from a time immemorial, it keeps the student from confusing his or her response for the call itself. They have some control over their responses, the personal commitments they make to alleviating suffering and pain in the world. But they do not have control over the ethical call itself, the call to responsibility.

So the student will not know exactly what the ethical call requires. That is, he or she cannot discern this rationally, consciously, cognitively. The knowledge learned in school falls short of this. There is a gap between call and response. The responses will be multiple, finite, historical, changeable, contextualized by concrete social and cultural situations. No teacher can tell them how to respond. The gap between call and response stops teachers from issuing clarion-clear blueprints to students about what to do to. For then students wouldn't themselves have to listen to the call, as the teacher would have done that for them. All students would have to do is go about the business of carrying out the preconceived plan of someone else. No, the gap between call and response, the call that comes to the students through the other others, constitutes a clear hesitation. To hear the call, to feel the lag between call and response, opens up a space to listen to those who suffer. It creates—in the student—a radical passivity that constitutes the ethical nature of being responsible. Learning animated by the teacher as other is simultaneously conditioned by an ethical call from society and the world, something students feel directly as a call. That is, the inspired learner is also a responsible subject.

In this chapter I have tried to indicate a different way to understand the conditions of the process of learning. In doing so, I have interpreted those conditions as connected to the ethical call to responsibility and the inspiration of hope. My aim was to offer an interpretation of learning that reveals its transcendent conditions. In the next chapter I attempt to do the same for the process of teaching and the relationship of the teacher to the student.

3
Teaching

Abstract: *A parallel to the previous chapter, this one addresses teaching and the teacher. It develops the Levinasian framework in terms of the teacher's subjectivity, traditionally construed as an autonomous subject embodying rationally developed disciplinary knowledge. Below that autonomy, the subjectivity of the teacher is a call to responsibility that comes through the student other, that is, as a unique person. This call acts as a regulatory function that appears as a structural responsibility for the teacher.*

Keywords: autonomy; hope; Levinas; responsibility; teacher; teaching

Joldersma, Clarence W. *A Levinasian Ethics for Education's Commonplaces: Between Calling and Inspiration.* New York: Palgrave Macmillan, 2014. DOI: 10.1057/9781137415493.0007.

In this chapter I describe the relation of teacher to student. At its deepest a teacher's subjectivity, like that of the student, is constituted through an intersubjective relation. Although from the perspective of the student the teacher is the other who inspires, the reverse relation, that of the teacher to the student, is not one of inspiration. The transcendent that conditions the teacher's subjectivity is a call to responsibility, one that comes through the student as other. This call acts as an ethical orientation that appears as a structural obligation to the student. This call is asymmetrical.

The teacher as autonomous

In the autonomy tradition, it is logical to understand the teacher as an adult autonomous subject. In this section I develop this idea by returning to discussions about consciousness, knowledge, and freedom, this time in connection to the teacher.

Consciousness is a difficult conceptual problem (Chalmers, 1997; Thompson, 2010) and I do not intend resolving it here. Consciousness is not immaterial, as Descartes argued, but is always already embodied. Nevertheless, to be embodied is to have a certain independence from our surroundings, something Levinas calls hypostasis (Levinas, 1987, p. 43). The metaphor of folding can help explain this term. Imagine reality to be like a large linen sheet, spread out. This is bare existence, which Levinas calls *il y a*, usually translated as "there is." Now imagine that at a local spot of bare existence a wrinkle appears and begins to fold into itself. The folding becomes so severe that the linen sheet tears at the outer edges of the fold. The result is a folded entity distinct from the simple, bare linen sheet. What emerges is an existent, a localized particular entity that, because of the folds, is in contact with itself. Hypostasis is the process of bare existence folding back onto itself and tearing away the rest of the "there is," creating a concrete location of subjectivity.

Hypostasis gives rise to consciousness. Humans as conscious beings are hypostatic existents arising out of the sea of bare existence. Out of the impersonal bare existence emerges a sheltering interiority that constitutes the subjectivity of consciousness. This makes the emergence of consciousness a form of freedom. This is not yet freedom of rational choice or conscious judgment, but the freedom of conscious independence from one's milieu within which one, nevertheless, still bathes.

The freedom that emerges is a conscious grip on existing in the face of impersonal forces that continually undermine it. Consciousness is not a bodiless spirit flying high above material existence; rather it is the continual effort to maintain a sheltering interiority in the face of continual decline.

Consciousness thus describes a certain kind of distance from the material elements upon which the emerging subject undoubtedly also very much depends. This relative independence shows up in the primordial experience of enjoyment. What makes me a subject, before any cognitive intentionality, is my awareness of enjoying what I live from. The joy brought on by the warmth of the sun on a lovely spring day or the pleasantness of the taste of a bite of fresh bread suggests a certain independence from those elements. Enjoyment is conscious awareness emerging as the subject gains some distance from the elements in which it is embedded. Consciousness involves the independence and freedom of enjoyment.

The distance of independence that marks consciousness means that it is characterized by intentionality. Consciousness is directed outward—it is *about* something. In the enlightenment tradition, this has been construed as developing adequate mental representations of reality (Aquila, 1983; Kant, 1999). Adequation involves a correspondence between representation and object. In a Levinasian construal, the conscious subject develops an adequate grasp of something, comprehending it as an object, encircling it with a concept, coming to possess it through conceptualization. The process of conceptualization is a domestication—getting something wild under control, making the strange familiar, bringing home what is foreign. This is an extension of hypostasis, where the intentionality of consciousness extends the subject's grip on existing in the face of unruly forces—an extension of independence and freedom. This is deliberate control by the conscious subject over a known object, accomplished by producing a neutral cognitive intermediary, a mental representation. This is the subject's power to grasp—comprehend—the world. At the same time, consciousness is to be continually present to the self we call the conscious subject. It is a vigilance constantly aware that it constitutes a rupture in the anonymity of bare existence (Levinas, 1995). In that rupture, consciousness forms a robust and insular self-presence while simultaneously being an intentional arrow that points outside itself, into the world. As self-present, it draws the world into its interiority. Intentionality is thus not so much an added function of consciousness, but its very core. To be a conscious subject is to be cognizant of the world as present in consciousness. The relation to the objective world is consciousness itself—intentionality is the way the world appears to the subject in the present.

The teacher can rightly be characterized as a conscious subject. From this angle, central to the teacher's subjectivity is autonomy, marked by independence and freedom. The teacher as autonomous embodies the ideals of intellectual activity and reasoning, someone who has made the knowledge of the world into his or her own. As autonomous, teachers have a grasp of reality, having domesticated the unruliness and messiness of the world by comprehending it. They embody the possibility of taming, through the clarity and distinctness of representations, external reality's strangeness and foreignness. As conscious subjects, teachers have mastered the indeterminate mysteries and unwelcome surprises of what is exterior to mind. Central to their mental representations is the arrow of intentionality that takes possession of the world cognitively, bringing it inside, making it a possession. Knowledge is present in the teacher's sheltering interiority.

This is central to the autonomy we can associate with the teacher. The teacher as autonomous subject possesses something foreign that has been domesticated through the meaning-giving of rational thought (Levinas, 1998a, p. 59). Thinking is an exercise of autonomy, creating independence from the world. Thought as meaning-giving to the world continually reestablishes the stability of the conscious subject as autonomous. Teachers are adults who embody this stability through their grasp of bodies of knowledge that constitute various aspects of the world. That knowledge is never just abstract and anonymous, but is centered in persons. In school, that person is the teacher. The teacher as autonomous embodies the adequation of thought and world; their mental representations correspond to external realities. But such adequation also shows the independence of the conscious subject precisely through such representation. Rather than being overwhelmed by the world, through representation the conscious subject keeps distance from it, maintaining the stability of the ego. The teacher as conscious subject is autonomous.

This model of the teacher's subjectivity has much to offer. We do rightly expect the identity of teachers to include self-control and reasoned judgment. And teachers in schools rightly should possess bodies of knowledge typically associated with academic disciplines and curricular subject areas. However, modeling the teacher's subjectivity as autonomous does not yet address his or her relation to a student, let alone how that relation can be construed as ethical. My argument will be that teaching, at its deepest is an ethically oriented intersubjective relation to a learner. This relationship situates the autonomy of the teacher. In particular, my claim will be that the teacher's freedom in autonomy is ethically oriented by a heteronomous relationship to the student, one that I characterize as the call to responsibility.

The responsible subject

The notion of autonomy is ultimately inadequate to mark the ethical orientation of the teacher in his or her relation to the student. In this section I will develop the idea that, below the autonomous subject, there is a deeper subjectivity. This subjectivity is inherently intersubjective, involving a relationship where the other is in a position of transcendence. The deeper subjectivity of the teacher, from a first-person perspective, involves an ethical disruption felt as responsibility. This ethically orients the teacher's relation to the student.

The autonomy model cannot adequately account for the deeper ethical relation. As autonomous, teachers are the same, and thus interchangeable. And students as (potential) autonomous subjects are (potential) alter egos of the teacher. They are interchangeable as equivalent voices of reason. The voice of reason is not personal, but universally substitutable (Biesta, 2004, p. 317). As conscious, cognitive subjects, teachers are individual instances of a common rational voice. Students are similarly interchangeable rational learners. The embodiment of rationally developed representations of a discipline's knowledge means that teachers and students, possessors or learners of that knowledge, are individual tokens of knowledge holders. Because they possess fundamentally the same knowledge, any one of them can easily substitute for any other. An ethical relationship of teacher to student does not appear through the subjectivity of rationally developed disciplinary knowledge or through the autonomy of self-control. The sameness of the interlocutors precludes this.

Rather, the ethical orientation associated with teaching emerges in a concrete, particular encounter with the student as other. In the encounter, Levinas offers, the other is immediately present. The other in this encounter is not an instance of a type—that is, a (potential) autonomous subject, similar to the teacher. The immediacy of the encounter means that the teacher does not have the space to use rational categories to identity the other as an alter ego. Rather the other shows up outside of all the teacher's categories. The other appears to the subject outside of all of the teacher's classification schemes, as a concrete singularity. A singularity is a concrete something that is not in a category, not even as an individual instance of that category. Instead, singularity refers to the individual beyond being categorized, as an extreme particular, one that shows up before the possibility of categorization. In the encounter with a student, at this level, the teacher is in relation with the student as a singularity before the teacher can categorize the student as a potential fellow rational, autonomous subject.

The singularity of the student as other makes him or her unique. Uniqueness is not mere difference, but irreplaceability. The uniqueness of the other gives him or her ethical worth, something Levinas calls "the dignity of the unique" (Levinas, 1998f, p. 194). The student's worth as other shows up before he or she is identified by the teacher as a (potential) member of the category "autonomous subject," but already in being irreplaceable. The highest dignity of the other is revealed in the other's concrete irreplaceability, something that arises in the concrete encounter with the other. The lack of criteria to identify the other in the encounter indicates that the relation is not cognitive. And the dignity associated with the uniqueness of the student as other, as irreplaceable, indicates that the teacher's relationship is in the realm of the ethical.

In the relationship with the student as other, the teacher is not a rational subject. Rather a deeper subjectivity emerges, precisely because the student as *other* is singular, unique. Central is the teacher's inability to decline the relationship—there is something inescapable about it. The immediacy of the encounter simultaneously signals its inescapability. One way to decline a relationship is to call in a substitute, someone who can replace oneself in the encounter. But in the inability to decline the relation, the teacher also shows up as being unique, that is, irreplaceable in the relation. This uniqueness is experienced, according to Levinas, as an ethical relation. In particular, Levinas states, "to be I signifies not being able to escape responsibility" (Levinas, 1996, p. 17). In the encounter, the teacher's deeper subjectivity emerges as an inescapable feeling of responsibility toward the student. The teacher feels irreplaceable in that obligation to the student—the irreplaceability singularizes the teacher. This is not a responsibility voluntarily shouldered by an interchangeable rational subject, but something that constitutes a deeper subjectivity of the teacher. No amount of wriggling and squirming can get the teacher as subject out of this responsibility. At this level, there is no such thing as a substitute teacher.

The felt responsibility that emerges for the teacher comes as a call. It comes as a summons from the student as other, disturbing the interiority of the teacher as an autonomous subject. Coming as a foreign disturbance, the call that arises through the encounter reveals a heteronomous subjectivity beneath the teacher's autonomy. To use a grammar metaphor, it reveals that below the teacher's nominative "I" of autonomy is the accusative "me" of heteronomy. The unsubstitutable "me" thus revealed shows itself as the affect of personal responsibility to the student as other. This is not a cognitive judgment. Rather it is an ethical call revealed through the encounter with the student as singularity, uncovering the subjectivity of the teacher as unsubstitutably responsible. The asymmetric encounter of the teacher to the student radically personalizes the teacher as a responsible subject.

In this section I have been developing a view of the teacher's subjectivity in his or her teaching relation. I have described a deeper subjectivity, one that emerges below that of autonomy, in which the teacher's relation is one of irreplaceable personal responsibility to the student as singular other. The teacher as responsible subject gives an ethical orientation to the teaching relation.

The asymmetry of teaching

The ethical call of responsibility grounds the process of teaching. This distinguishes the conditions for teaching from those of learning. One way to distinguish the two sorts of conditions—one for learning and another for teaching—is by returning to the contrast between calling and inspiration. The previous section developed the idea of being called to responsibility. The distinction between calling and inspiration forms the basis for distinguishing between the ethical orientations of teaching and learning. From the perspective of the learner, where the teacher is the other, the student is inspired; from the perspective of the teacher where the student is other, the teacher is called. The difference between the notions of call and inspiration gives a clear articulation of the ethical orientation of each relationship. The difference in the relationship to the other makes the asymmetrical relation of the teacher to the student different from that of the student to the teacher.

Teaching is something that occurs in many kinds of social institutions as well as outside of them. Although my focus here is on the teaching located within specialized institutions we name colleges and high schools, it applies to teaching generally. And although it is not incorrect to view teaching as a set of techniques, my aim is to set out the ethical orientation that conditions those methods, namely, the subjectivity of the teacher in his or her relation to the student. And it is as ethical orientation that the idea of a reciprocal relation is most clearly inadequate. In the relationship with the student, the teacher is someone who feels a call coming from elsewhere, through the student as other. The relationship is unidirectional, *from* the student *to* the teacher, and not the reverse. Although clearly intersubjective, the teacher's relationship to the student is asymmetrical because the ethical call comes from the student as other, a summons that reveals the teacher to be a responsible subject.

One way to mark that asymmetry is, following Levinas's idiom, to highlight that for the fact that for the teacher the student is the *other*. In the previous section I developed the idea that in the encounter the student as other appears as unique, a singularity. As a result, the subjectivity of the teacher is marked by a call to responsibility. The responsibility involved can be further described using Levinas's ideas of *face* and *neighbor*. As a *face*, the student as singular other shows up as pure vulnerability and exposedness. Clearly, at a cognitive level for the teacher, students come with obvious agendas and strengths, not to mention defenses and obnoxiousness. However, in the ethical encounter, the learner as other is characterized by a profound defenselessness—a *face* according to Levinas. Central to the asymmetry is the fact that in the relationship, precisely in the moment of teaching, the student is vulnerable and exposed. Levinas's notion of *neighbor* adds to this. The neighbor is someone who I didn't choose to be a friend or companion, who doesn't necessarily have my voluntary love. The neighbor also is exposed to the arbitrariness that comes from the whims of the powerful, sovereign *I* who is free and independent. Being a neighbor marks the inescapable character of the obligation. Designating the learner as other in terms of neighbor connotes someone who is inescapably in the life of the teacher.

Precisely because the learner as other is exposed and vulnerable and yet is my neighbor, the neighbor's face is a commanding force, a *call* to me. The face is the ethical call 'thou shalt not kill' or more positively, 'do me good.' Precisely because in the teaching relation the learner as other is vulnerable and exposed, without protection, it gives an ethical call of responsibility, namely, the summons to do no harm. To be faced with the face of the learner is to be called to do the learner good. No word need be spoken, no by-law put into a faculty handbook, no utility calculated by an institution, no principle invoked by a state: the very face-to-face encounter with the learner as other calls the teacher to do the learner good. The very face of the learner as other reveals the potential arbitrariness of the teacher's knowledge and plans for the course, the claim to know exactly what is needed in the course based on long study, with respect to that particular student. That is, the face puts into question the teacher's autonomy and freedom.

Thus, what ethically orients the act of teaching is the responsibility to and for the student. This responsibility is not first a task—perhaps one of many on a 'to do' list—that an instructor has. Instead, it is an asymmetric transcendent condition for all the acts of teaching we might devise. At its deepest, teaching is ethically oriented by responsibility to and for the student as other; responsibility comprises the deepest core of the teacher's subjectivity, the teacher is a responsible subject. The heteronomy of responsibility defines the subjectivity of the teacher before his or her autonomy of freedom.

In the student's vulnerability and exposedness, the autonomy of the teacher is curtailed, giving the learner protection. This means that the student as other is outside the purview of the teacher, outside his or her conceptualizing grasp, out of reach of the extending circle of the teacher's own freedom. To be inside that sphere would make the student a mere extension of the teacher, perhaps part of that person's urge for self-preservation and enjoyment, a prop in the teacher's freedom and autonomy. Or, to be inside that circle might be to make the learner a function of the institution or the world economic system, of which the teacher is always inevitably a representative. For example, we might view the purpose of teaching to make the student become like the teacher as much as possible, in terms of knowledge, skills, behaviors, habits, tendencies, attitudes, beliefs. Of course, no teacher or school would wish the learner to imitate the arbitrary or idiosyncratic aspects of the teacher. Yet, the extent to which the teacher embodies an objective set of knowledge, skills and dispositions—perhaps as a universal representative of a discipline such as biology—to that degree we often think that the student ought to become like the teacher.

In the model that I'm proposing, the student, as *other*, is outside of the teacher's circle, external to the encompassing temptation for the teacher in his or her autonomy. The student as learner calls for responsibility on the part of the teacher to do the student no harm, to do him or her good. This call to responsibility is not a call to develop rationality or economically competitive human capital. This re-situates the call within the circle of the teacher as representative of rationality or an economic world order. Instead, the call to responsibility comes directly from the person with whom one is face to face, the student as learner. And not to the student whom we are trying to make like us, as a rational, knowledgeable, economically ready creature, but to the student as other, beyond that inevitable urge for self-reproduction by the teacher as representative of reason and society, of national pride or neo-liberal economies. Teaching at its deepest is conditioned by an ethical orientation that comes in the form of an ethical call to responsibility to the student as other. This is the asymmetry of teaching.

Called to teach

In this section I will connect the ethical orientation more directly to the act of teaching. In the previous sections I argued that the teacher's subjectivity involves being called to responsibility to the student as other. In an earlier chapter I described the ethical call as coming from beyond memory, from a time immemorial. That means something beyond the memorable past, the past as it can be represented in the present, becoming fully present. The ethical call has something to do with hearing something we are not in position to hear, since we were not present when it came. That is, the call has to do with hearing what is actually impossible to hear—a trace. Rather, it is felt as an ethical obligation, a responsibility.

The call to teach is deeper than autonomy. It comes to a teacher from beyond his or her freedom, from the other that is outside the teacher's control, on the other side of his or her circle of autonomy. The call that comes from the face of the student reverberates with the enigma of the ethical, coming from a time immemorial, before the teacher is ready to respond. Teachers, precisely in their teaching function, have no recourse to adjust it more to their liking, for call from a time immemorial is beyond the teacher's grasp, out of reach of his domesticating memory, her representing ability. A teacher's deep passivity arising from the call is felt as his or her concrete responsibility to the student as other, as a neighbor, which is evidence of the ethical character of that call. It is evidence that the call to responsibility frames teaching with a particular ethical orientation. Whereas learning primarily involves the passivity of inspiration and reverberating with hope, teaching involves the ethics of responsibility. The call to teach is ethical, but its ethical nature is revealed as responsibility in actions.

Teaching involves lecturing, organizing lab activities, assigning readings, asking questions, leading discussions, assessing papers, assigning grades. It is tempting to argue—based on the previous chapter's discussion of learning—that the ethics of these teaching methods is to be a disturbing and surprising presence that, nevertheless, is welcomed by the student. But this is not the ethical orientation of *teaching*. Although it is true that from the student's point of view learning involves welcoming these as disturbances, this does not simply transfer to the teacher's point of view; the two asymmetrical relationships are different from each other. The ethical orientation for teaching is not aimed at disrupting the student's (misplaced, naïve, simplistic, inadequate) understanding of something. Instead, from the teacher's perspective, any disruption of the student must itself be guided by an ethical orientation. Teaching is conditioned by the call of the face, the face's command to do the student good.

It is important to note that the call comes through the face of the student. This implies that the call does not come from the parents, or the school board, or the legislature, or business leaders, or school reformers—no, it comes through the student him or herself. And this is not some verbal exchange with the student, as if the student is conscious and deliberate about putting in this call to the teacher—a phone call, say, before class—no, the call comes precisely through the face of the student, that is, the student as other. It manifests itself directly in the concrete relationship between teacher and learner.

One view of doing a student good might be articulated using a health metaphor. Sometimes a parent suggests that a child take some medicine for its own good; that despite possible distaste for the process and lack of insight by the recipient, the result is for the good of the child. By analogy, one might be tempted to suggest that precisely because students are shortsighted they need the wisdom of others who know better and can see farther, and thus have the right (if not the duty) to force onto students certain knowledge and dispositions and skills for their own good, despite possible protestations. On this model, as long as the teacher's actions are legitimated by good reasons and sanctioned by others—school boards, reformers, business leaders, legislators—who claim to be in a good position to judge, then the student's own position becomes irrelevant to whether or not the action is for the good of the student or whether it harms the student. But this construal of doing good is a function of something other than the student as other.

There is, of course, much truth in these ideas. Certainly it is true that students themselves do not really *know* what is good for them. For example, often students complain about long, difficult readings, or about lessons that seem irrelevant to them. Students often rejoice at the cancellation of a class if the professor has to be away to a conference or if the high school is closed because of a winter snowstorm. These and other things suggest that students do not always know what is good for them. Students are nearsighted in this regard. And how could it be otherwise? To be a student is precisely to be shortsighted. Schools are rightly designed to make students more farsighted, to give them a bigger perspective on themselves and the world. If teaching is disruption, then student's shortsightedness is one of the casualties of such interruption. In that sense, schooling is rightly a good, albeit sometimes bitter, medicine.

But the call from student to teacher comes from a depth beyond the health metaphor. Although schooling may well involve a health model from the perspective of the student, that doesn't yet make it into an ethical orientation from the perspective of the teacher. The two relationships aren't symmetrical. As a teacher I do not choose my students, yet I am in an inescapable relationship of responsibility to and for them. This ethical orientation directs me to a 'must accept them as they are,' even when and if they turn out not to be the example of learner that I think would be ideal for my class. They remain my students—irreplaceably—even when they don't do as I ask, when they come late to class or miss assignments, when they read poorly and or have difficulty grasping the concepts so clearly presented in class. What orients all these things ethically is the call to responsibility that comes through the student, the face of the student as other: 'do me good.' The face of the student—the exposure and vulnerability beyond its visible characteristics—creates an obligation that comes before the teacher can limit it and remains larger than he or she can adequately discharge. The teacher is in an asymmetric ethical relation with the student, one that the teacher cannot escape and one that seems to have no end in sight.

Now, this rightly seems excessive. If teachers take this ethical orientation seriously, they would be working all day, every day, all year long, non-stop. Many do. That rightly undermines the well-being of teachers—viewing the ideal teacher in terms of extreme self-sacrifice undermines the teacher's own flourishing as a professional (Higgins, 2011). Clearly teachers need to take care of their own well-being in order to last in the profession. As autonomous individuals, they need to decide how much to sacrifice without 'burning out.' But those deliberate, cognitively inflected actions themselves speak to an underlying call that ceaselessly obligates teachers in their teaching. An analogous call in parenting makes this clear. Responsible parents recognize that their obligation to their children is an ethical call that they can never escape and which seems to have no end in sight. And the call comes through the mere existence of the child, not in anything he or she says or does or achieves. There are no strings attached, no contractual limits. I'm suggesting that an analogous call is present in teaching. Underneath the requirement to take care of one's mental health by limiting one's work as a teacher is the very real infinite nature of the responsibility of the teacher to the students in his or her life. The ethical call to responsibility is excessive.

What this means at least is that each student is not expendable. No student as other can be neglected or abandoned. Each is unique: irreplaceable. The call that comes through the face of the student for a teacher means that he or she is obligated to do good to *that* student. This means two things. First, it means that *that particular* teacher is obligated. In the ethical call there is no such thing as a substitute teacher. Just as the good Samaritan was not able to look over his shoulder and gesture to the wounded man, 'there is someone else coming who will take care of you, I'm going to be late for my meeting in Jericho and I am not responsible for you' so too a particular teacher is not able to gesture over his shoulder with the message that there's a substitute coming who will discharge his responsibility to the student. No, the ethical orientation means there is no such thing as a substitute teacher. The responsibility is part of the teacher's very subjectivity, inescapably. Second, it means the teacher is obligated to *that* student. In the teaching relation, that particular student is irreplaceable. Despite all those who tried and perhaps failed to get into the class—the teacher is popular after all—she cannot merely substitute another student for the one that faces her now. Central to the transcendence that ethically conditions the teacher-to-student relation is that this particular student calls the teacher to teach, and not just to teach in general, but to teach *that* student particularly.

Now, some may argue that this is over the top. After all, don't teachers rightly have office hours, class times, grading scales, semester-long courses, standards for maintaining academic standing, graduation requirements? Don't these signal that institutionally a limited collective and individual sense of obligation to the students? Yes and no. I will argue in Chapter 5 that institutionalization is both a limitation on a teacher's obligations and a concrete way to balance his or her many responsibilities. However, here my main emphasis is that the teacher's ethical relation to the student is deeper, more primary. Institutional structure provides a context for the actual interaction between teacher and student. Although institutionalization is ubiquitous in any modern society, teaching itself doesn't require many of the things that are essential to institutional life as institutions.

Take the phenomenon of assessment as an example. Successful teaching does not require grades. Some teachers believe in the opposite, that grades are essential, perhaps for motivation or to signal adequate mastery of the material. I disagree. Although good teaching may well include feedback on what is learned, it doesn't require the summative evaluation that grades are meant to mark. Using grades for motivation is extraneous to the actual task of teaching. Parents, for example, don't assign grades to their children, either for motivation or for evaluation, and, nevertheless, much teaching occurs in parenting, including continuous feedback. Further, teachers often complain about the oft-repeated question: is this going to be on the test? But that question indicates something external to the act of teaching that sets the agenda for the students. Reporting a grade is extraneous to teaching. When only two people are involved, a teacher and a student, the act of teaching involves continual, direct feedback, and can do without grades.

Similar arguments can be made for almost all the structures that are typically associated with teaching found in formal schooling. The institutionalization of teaching is not at the same level as the direct ethical obligation of the teacher to the student. My point here is not to say that institutionalization is illegitimate, or that we should eliminate these finely honed structures. Institutional contexts create a dedicated space for teaching that would be difficult to duplicate. Instead, I'm merely pointing out that in the ethical orientation that conditions the teaching relation, institutionalization is something external to a teacher's direct obligation to his or her student. As an ethical relation this responsibility is limitless, unending, something that cannot in itself be discharged through the activity of teaching. This excess reveals institutionalization as setting conventional limits, from the outside, on the otherwise unending obligatory relation.

The call that comes through the student disrupts the autonomy of the teacher. From a certain angle, we can construe the structures that institutionalize education as giving a certain amount of control over teaching. Rules, regulations, expectations, objectives, consequences, plans, and so forth, all regularize the teaching so that it is predictable and controllable. In the institutional context, the call that comes through the face of the student comes as a disruptive force of those structures. The call to responsibility interrupts the well-crafted set of institutional regulations that mark formal schooling. And it is as a disruptive force that teachers most visibly feel the call to responsibility. A student interrupts a clearly developed lesson with a question that is only tangentially related. An answer to a question in an exam clearly shows signs of learning, just not the material that was asked for by the test question. A student disrupts a fine conversation among teachers during morning coffee to ask about a reading. These obvious interruptions, I think, point to something deeper. What makes them interruptions is that they bring to the immediate surface the call to responsibility, something that often is buried beneath the more obvious visibility of institutionalization. They bring to the foreground the ethical orientation that inescapably is the relation between teacher and student: this particular teacher and that particular student. As if no other student mattered. The call beckons as if the institution was not there, bracketed from consideration. The call to responsibility breaks through with a disruptive force.

But this means that the institutional context cannot extinguish, although it may curtail or even hide the asymmetric ethical relationship exposed by the face of the student. Institutionalization cannot completely eliminate that the student is the teacher's neighbor. Sometimes teachers argue that this call happens once, at the beginning of their career, in which they have taken stock of their talents and matched them to certain needs in society: 'I am called to become a teacher.' However, the relationship I'm naming the call to teach is something that occurs again and again. Each time someone enters a teaching relationship, each time one steps into a classroom, each time one teaches a lesson, each time the teacher questions a student, the call emerges from the face of the student. Inescapably. The call to teach shows up every time a student asks a teacher a question, each time the teacher makes one of the hundreds of tiny decisions they make every day, every week, every semester. It is a call that never fades or, more accurately, one that is continually renewed.

What I'm arguing in this section is that professional teachers, those associated with formal, institutionalized schooling, are ethically oriented in their teaching by a distinctive call. The call to teach is, at its deepest, being called to responsibility directly through the face of the student, as other.

The inspiration to hope animating justice

The previous sections argued that the transcendent call to responsibility conditions the everyday activities of teaching. However, this does not yet address the outward-oriented aim of education, one whose goal is contributing to the good of society. That involves explicating another ethical relation that conditions teaching. This one orients teaching outward, beyond the confines of the immediacy of the classroom, beyond the call to responsibility to the student.

Both the call to responsibility and the inspiration to hope, we discussed in Chapter 1, show up here and now in the concrete call that comes through the marginalized in society and around the globe. This links responsibility and inspiration to justice. The call of justice, as it comes through the marginalized people in society, provides an overarching reason for teaching our students. The teacher's relationship to the student as other is itself set in a wider context, one that in the previous chapter I termed *other others*. The wider context for teaching is ultimately the possible actions by students with respect to the marginal and voiceless members of society and the vulnerable and fragile ecosystems that we inhabit.

A teacher's obligation to the student as other is set in a context of a broader hope. A teacher's obligation to the student is not situated in an education geared to developing the student into an autonomous rational subject per se. Instead, an equally primordial, though less immediately apparent, condition for teaching is the inspiration of justice, the hope that human flourishing will come to the poor, the weak, the underemployed. The teacher's obligation to the student is itself oriented by an ethical inspiration of real possibilities for the other others in the world around us who cannot advocate for themselves. Teaching fundamentally is also grounded in something outside of the student, in the other others, in the disruptive affect of hope for the world. This does not come through the student as other directly, but through the other others in society. Hope for the world relativizes teaching goals such as academic excellence, personal development, and finding truth. Teaching is inspired by the other others, which shows up as a hope for justice in the world that conditions the immediate acts of teaching.

The hopefulness of this hope is not first for the student but for the world. Hope for the refugee, the war victim, the underemployed; for vulnerable ecologies and decimated resources. The very act of teaching signals that these situations are not hopeless, that present inequalities and behaviors are not ironclad. Teaching, conditioned by social hope, is grounded in a time unforeseen, as can be seen in its implicit suggestion that the present situation of the other others is not the way it ought to be and that it can be better, here and now. Teaching that embodies hope is oriented toward real possibilities of doing public good wherever things are not the way they ought to be. Teaching conditioned by hope shows up as the animated by justice.

Teaching animated by justice is tied to the desire for something new to break through, in spite of present circumstances. Teaching involves longing for a genuinely different situation, quite dissimilar to the present but in the present. More strongly, teaching is an expectation that the present will be ruptured by peace and justice, delight and joy. Teaching is a disbelief in the ironclad continuity of the present lack of human flourishing due to injustice.

The inspiration to hope doesn't just come from anywhere. It ultimately comes from beyond vision, from a time unforeseeable, albeit through the other others: the stranger, alien, widow, orphan, prisoner, outcast—in society and around the globe. The orientation of the teacher inspired in this manner is to be disturbed by otherness. Such inspiration marks being affected by the suffering and pain of those other others, not being able to evade being affected by the injustice, oppression, and marginalization. Being inspired as a teacher is to be motivated by something beyond the student, beyond the institution, beyond the community, in and for the world. For the sake of teaching the student. For the good of the student as other. In recognition that the others in the world are other others for the student too.

Evidence for such hope shows up, here and now, in the form of a teacher's inspiration. It shows up in the present in the teacher's non-indifference to the pain and suffering of the other others in the world in the very process of teaching. Hope occurs in the present here in the form of a teacher's inability to be non-indifferent to the plight of those around. Hope, the belief that difficult situations can and must be changed, animates the teacher beyond the student even as he or she is obligated to that student. A teacher's hope, in this sense, is located in the world yet is outside of its causal structure. That hope involves believing the impossible is possible, as if a breach in causality is possible, in the present. The interruption of hope takes the form of the teacher's impossibility to remain indifferent. Inspiration motivates the teacher to orient teaching in a direction that realistically he or she has no real business believing will make a difference.

In this chapter I have connected the process of teaching to two transcendental conditions, inspiration and hope. Our understanding of the teaching must be oriented by the call to responsibility. But it must also be connected to the world through the hope of justice. In so doing, for teachers working at formal institutions of schooling, the very process of teaching itself contributes to justice in society.

4 Curriculum

Abstract: *This chapter addresses the curriculum using the Levinasian ethics developed earlier. It first articulates the representational model of knowledge typically connected to an understanding of curricular content and then reinterprets this within a Levinasian frame. The analysis suggests that the representational model is inadequate for understanding curricular knowledge, and the chapter supplements it with the Levinasian ideas of listening and tactful touch. These concepts unsettle the perception of a finished character of the knowledge associated with the curriculum and its concomitant compartmentalization into the disciplines. This reinterpretation invites seeing curriculum as truthful disclosure of the world in ways beyond representation and gives the teacher a function of trusteeship. This analysis follows Levinas's suspicion of totalizing understanding of curriculum, unsettling its disciplinary confinement and encyclopedic comprehension.*

Keywords: ethics; Levinas; representationalism; unsuspected horizons

Joldersma, Clarence W. *A Levinasian Ethics for Education's Commonplaces: Between Calling and Inspiration.* New York: Palgrave Macmillan, 2014. DOI: 10.1057/9781137415493.0008.

The previous two chapters were analyses of two of education's commonplaces, teaching and learning. Although participants in formal schooling rightly see themselves as teaching and learning, these are always *about* something. One never just teaches or learns, for there is always *something* that is taught and learned. That something involves the third educational commonplace, the curriculum. In this chapter I reinterpret the representational model of knowledge typically connected to our understanding of curricular content. My analysis suggests that the representational model is inadequate for understanding curricular knowledge, and I introduce the ideas of listening and tactful touch to supplement it. These concepts unsettle the perception of a finished character of the knowledge associated with the curriculum and its concomitant compartmentalization into the disciplines. My reinterpretation invites seeing curriculum as truthful contact with the world in ways beyond representation. This analysis utilizes Levinas's suspicion of totality to resist reducing curriculum to its disciplinary confinement and encyclopedic comprehension.

The curriculum is typically differentiated into various formal divisions. In secondary and tertiary schooling these include areas such as the natural sciences, the social sciences, the humanities, and the arts. They are popularly called subjects, with names such as English, biology, history, geography, mathematics, home economics, industrial arts, computer science, physical education. Each area has its own peculiar structure and dynamic, which makes it difficult to generalize about curriculum without doing some injustice to the particularity of each one. Yet, we do call it by a singular collective: the curriculum. At times I will generalize, ignoring the particularities of specific areas, while at other times I will capitalize on the particulars of an area to illuminate more general points. My aim is to situate the curriculum in the ethical call and the inspiration to hope, thereby giving the content of what is learned and taught an ethical orientation that aligns itself with a justice-directed construal of education.

Curriculum as representational knowledge

Especially in secondary and tertiary schooling, teachers typically identify the curriculum with the content of their courses. The curriculum is then said to constitute the knowledge that shows up in their courses, which we can construe broadly enough to include skills and dispositions. Although talk of content might more typically be associated with areas of the curriculum such the social or natural sciences, the arts and humanities can also be thought of in those terms. Despite obvious and real differences between the various areas, underlying the curriculum is a pervasive, if tacit, understanding of what constitutes knowledge.

It embodies a view that can be called a representationalist model of knowledge (Aquila, 1983). In that model, a person knows the external world by means of a set of mental representations. Representations are intermediaries between person and world, which make the un-thought world available. Instead of a direct, dyadic relation between person and world, this is a mediated relation, modeled as a triad of subject, world, and representation. When the representation satisfies particular rational or empirical requirements, then the representation is said to constitute knowledge about the world (Lynch, 2001). By being translated into an intermediary, a representation, we gain an adequate picture on the world. When the world is represented, human subjects extend their knowledge of the world. Representations are named in a variety of ways, including ideas, concepts, descriptions, observations, explanations, imaginings, predictions, models, theories, information, and facts. Collectively speaking, representations constitute the bodies of knowledge associated with the various areas of the curriculum.

One might object that this view of knowledge, though perhaps present in certain parts of the curriculum, is not the reigning model throughout. One can readily concede that the natural sciences embody a representationalist view. On this view, representations are modeled as theories and observations in physics, or as abstract mathematical formulations. With slight modification this view can add social sciences as constituted by representationalist knowledge, replete with facts, theories, and models. But, one might object, the humanities and especially the arts are not representational. Nor are subjects such as physical education, home economics, and industrial arts. These do not embody a representationalist view of knowledge. For example, the view that paintings are meant to represent reality is no longer the paradigm. And an exercise regime is not meant to be an attempt to represent reality.

This is a legitimate objection, and cannot be answered adequately without an extended discussion beyond the purview of the present chapter. But there are good historical and systematic reasons to think that the representational theory of knowledge is the model that gives the standard against which to measure the knowledge content of all areas of the curriculum, including the arts and humanities. For this to be plausible, we need to expand the notion of representation to include a broader swath of the curriculum without doing injustice to the representational model. Despite obvious differences with the natural and social sciences, the content of these other subjects, whether it involves interpreting poems and novels, writing compositions or producing sculptures and paintings, nevertheless, involves representations.

In Chapter 2 I pointed out that schooling typically views the student as a self-learner, something which equates learning with a move toward autonomy. On this account, the student gains control over self and the world via learning, which is often modeled through the formation of representations that gain control. This can be seen in some of the everyday events in schooling. The irritating student, who continually asks after every sparkling lesson whether 'this will be on the test,' is attempting to cope with his or her academic world, representing it by reducing the overwhelming amount of new material to a manageable level so that he or she can survive if not faintly enjoy the world of learning. This vexing question can be interpreted as an attempt by the student to control his or her world in the context of having little say. The student as subject acts as a rational agent trying to obtain maximum grip on the world, via representing it in certain ways for control and increased autonomy. Action in the world involves representing it in ways that give the person, as thinking subject, more control over the world within which he or she lives.

This example, however, is peripheral to the construal of the representational nature of curriculum as such. My argument is that the curriculum as a whole is implicitly interpreted as representational, a complement to understanding the student as autonomous. A student gains autonomy via mastery of the representational knowledge the curriculum affords. A representational construal of the curriculum is a counterpart to learning as cognitive intentionality and teachers as rational embodiments of disciplinary knowledge. Representation is implicit in these interpretations of the curriculum, before the more particular questions associated with individual subjects and disciplines come into play. On the autonomy model of schooling, representation forms the basis for the more concrete curricula particulars. We can put this in terms of what can be brought to mind, without remainder. In a representational understanding, the aim of student mastery of knowledge is successfully bringing to mind the knowledge that constitutes the curriculum. Nothing is left over in the successful act of knowing. Cognitive knowing is the central, paradigmatic act for learning in this model. The curriculum, the vehicle for knowing, is implicitly representational.

On this view, we can recover reality in memory without remainder. The idea of memory includes the intellectual representations humans have developed to portray reality. Put temporally, a representational view involves the interpretation that reality is something like a past that can always be remembered in the present, that is, re-presented. The order and patterns embedded in reality can always be, in principle, recuperated in a satisfactory manner. Below the surface of chaotic dynamics lies an underlying intelligible pattern that can be projected into the foreseeable future. Prediction, planning, and control all rely on this interpretation. To talk of knowledge in a representational view is to speak of explanation and prediction. These all exist within recoverable time by being representable.

Unsuspected horizons for representations

There is much to be said for the representationalist model of knowledge. In fact, we likely cannot do without it. My critique does not involve an analysis of the differences of representational models among the various disciplines of the curriculum. Nor does it attempt to adjudicate whether the social sciences, the arts, and the humanities ought to be modeled on the natural sciences. I think that these important discussions ultimately need the attention of those who work within these various areas. But it is my contention that such discussions are framed by a representational view of knowledge, something that pervades the dominant understanding of the curriculum generally. My critique centers on the representational model itself, with an eye to unsettling its privilege in the curriculum.

Understanding more fully the model of knowledge in play here requires exploring the interrelations among knowledge, world, and human subjectivity, beginning with the latter. Previous chapters described the human subject as the enjoying subject. The world, on this reading, is the surrounding elements, namely, the enjoyable nourishment that one takes in. The world is the bread in its tasty goodness, the sun in its feeling warm, the breeze in its felt freshness on the face, the touch in its experience as love, the music in its pleasantness, the discussion in its agreeableness, and the coming of an idea in its satisfaction. In short, the world is that which constitutes the enjoyed surroundings for the enjoying subject.

This experience of the world, as elements that provide joy for an enjoying subject, is not yet representational knowledge. The enjoyed world is too close to the subject as a sensible being to generate rational knowledge; the subject is *immersed* in the world. The world for the enjoying subject is the external pole of the feelings of joy: the world primordially is a series of elements that constitutes enjoyable nourishment for the enjoying subject. And if we take the idea of elements literally—that which cannot be broken down further—then there isn't much more to say about the world beyond the idea of its incoming sustenance of the enjoying subject. In particular, it can't be characterized in terms of knowledge as representational.

The enjoying subject is an independent subject. As embodied, the subject is free to move about in the world, and in the process continuously gathers sensorimotor information. Sensorimotor actions are intentional, enacted in the context of a meaningful world (Joldersma, 2013b). The world, as external surroundings, is beyond the subject while simultaneously affording mobility to the subject, the freedom to move within its environment. Such mobility suggests that the enjoying subject has freedom. There is a particular distance between subject and world, a gap without which enjoyment could not take place. Felt enjoyment indicates an implicit awareness of that gap, indicating an emergent independence from the world. This is a form of consciousness. Although not yet self-consciousness, let alone rational reflection, it is an awareness that ruptures the anonymity of the elements that constitute what exists—bare existence or the "there is." The anonymous reality is torn by a presence which is present to itself as an emerging subject. Subjectivity indicates a certain level of withdrawal from being totally immersed in the world. For example, enjoying the first bite of freshly baked bread spread with honey requires not being totally immersed in that activity, but having some awareness of the warmth of the bread in one's mouth and of the sweetness of the honey on the palate. That is, joy is also the experience of joy, being somewhat removed from the activity even while engaging in it. Without some distance, existent and bare existence would be one, and there is no subject. Although such awareness is of one's surroundings, it simultaneously does have an implicit, minimal self-awareness as well. This is, at least, the implicit awareness of the surroundings as not oneself, as different from oneself. The very feeling of enjoyment requires a minimal self-awareness in this way. This is a kind of self-presence, something that can become the crystallization point out of which more complex consciousness emerges. The continuity of these degrees of subjective awareness implies a relative degree of independence from the world via reflexivity.

The independence of the subject also indicates something else: freedom is not stable. To be independent is also to be vulnerable. Since as a bodily creature the subject is always dependent on the world, it can also succumb to the vicissitudes of the elements that temporarily sustain it. What if the nourishment supply were cut off? What if the incoming elements no longer nourished? Independence, precisely because of the joy associated with it, also feels continually threatened. Consciousness, including feeling the joy of the enjoyable, also feels this precariousness. We can easily imagine a young child worriedly protecting a bowl of ice-cream from a teasing parent precisely because the child is enjoying it so much. Or, more tragically, as the vulnerability and misery of those affected by Hurricane Katrina and Typhoon Haiyan can attest that the ordinary enjoyment of everyday life can be abruptly and easily disrupted. Even the angry student questioning a teacher's judgments about his or her grade can be construed as motivated by a worry caused by a sudden vulnerability to plans for college and medical school. Enjoyable freedom can be lost in a flash. The graciously sustaining earth is also perceived as constituted by forces and dynamics that can at any time threaten the independence of the subject. The sustaining earthly elements of bare existence also cause anxiety about the security of one's independence.

The anxiety about maintaining the independence of enjoyment in the face of threats brings into focus the conscious agency of the subject. Agency plausibly emerges in the face of danger. We can think of an idea of agency as a point of power in the human person that attempts to protect its freedom of enjoyment by controlling its surroundings to maintain its own survival. For example, such agency is visible when we construct buildings to maintain life-protecting micro-climates in the context of sweltering summer heat or raging winter blizzards. It is visible when a teacher develops a detailed syllabus laying out clear student expectations to ward off possible anxiety about being an incompetent instructor in order to gain job security. This view of agency can be construed as the power to organize the elements in the environment to maintain and enhance the stability of life as enjoyably independent of that threatening world. The agent is an embodied "I can" that has the ability to affect its surroundings for itself and its own longevity and well-being. Agency is that which protects 'my place in the sun.'

Human consciousness, on this reading, involves an intentional arrow directed toward the world. As centered, the conscious subject is originator of action directed toward the world for some particular purpose. Action in the world by the conscious subject is intentional, *about* something. For example, the intentionality involved in constructing a school's physical buildings is *about* protection from adverse climatic conditions and weather patterns. And the intentionality connected to writing a clear syllabus is in part *about* protection from adverse student reactions. Of course, those are not the only ways of warding off the threatening world in these settings, for a range of possible actions might do more or less adequately. As such, an intentional being might be thought of as a centered origin of a large number of possible actions to accomplish particular intentions.

Intentionality, as directed activity, is connected to coping and surviving in the world. Phrases such as 'experiment,' 'control,' 'come to grips with,' and having 'a grasp of the world' are all appropriate to name this construal of intentionality. Grasping something with the hand is central to knowing the world. Many of a baby's first directed motor actions are graspings; a child's tendency in trying to understand something is often to grab the entity with its hand. The prehensile hand is remarkably well suited for bodily knowing the world through grasping it (Wilson, 1999). Without the phenomenon of grasping there would likely be no full-blown bodily agency. As Levinas argues, "The hand delineates a world by drawing what it grasps from the element, delineating definite beings having forms, that is, solids; the informing of the formless is solidification, emergence of the graspable, the existent, support of qualities" (Levinas, 1969, p. 161). The hand is not merely a biological appendage, but a way of deliberately delineating the world. The beginnings of the representational knowledge relation to the world are based in the need to control, to come to grips with reality by delineating it. The hand is a hand in its ability to apprehend. It is its grasping and holding ability that constitutes its handiness. The hand leads in the intentional act.

That this is a central ground for the representational knowledge has been empirically and conceptually substantiated by Lakoff and Johnson (Lakoff, & Johnson, 1980, 1999). They suggest that there are certain basic metaphors that organize whole systems of concepts employed in theoretical knowledge, claiming that these concepts arise from our bodily action on our physical environment (Lakoff, & Johnson, 1980, p. 14). This gives us a way of modeling how conceptual, representational knowledge is possible, derived from bodily agency in the world. Our bodily way of dealing with the world generates certain basic bodily action-patterns, the stylized ways we bodily act on the world, from birth onward. The constraining patterns of bodily action form the core of representational knowledge. The agent's experimenting with things, controlling things, dealing with the world, coping with it, coming to grips with it, as conscious interactions with the world with the intention of survival and well-being, form the basis of representation knowledge. Human intentionality often involves capturing things in the world, grasping entities and constraining them in order to experiment, cope, or deal with the world. One can think of the "in-out" action associated with a container metaphor: when you have grasped something, your hand acts as a container. Metaphorically, the representational model of knowing can be understood as pulling something you want into a conceptual container. At the representational level, knowledge is something that one has grasped, precisely because it is conceptually pulled in. The representational model of knowing is grounded in the phenomenon of bodily grasping because conceptualization itself is a metaphorical form of grasping.

In Chapter 3 I argued that central to consciousness is intentionality. Levinas remarks, "Consciousness is always correlative with a theme, a present represented, a theme put before me, a being which is a phenomenon" (Levinas, 1998d, p. 25). Consciousness does not merely *use* intentionality, as if it were an external aid for its proper functioning, but is constituted as intentional. The intentional relation, concretely embodied in the hand delineating the world, is more abstractly the essence of consciousness. The agent's process of thematization is coming to grips with the world as conscious intentionality. Central to the notion of consciousness as intentionality is that it forms representations. Consciousness brings representations into presence, in the present. The formation of representations involves assembling various elements, including from short- and long-term memory, into a present synchronization (Levinas, 1998d, p. 140). The process of representation is not something in addition to conscious intentionality, but it is its very core. Cognitive intentionality *is* representation. It is the act of making present again in collected, synthetic form the subject's embodied interactions with the world. Consciousness is a way of relating to the world by representing it in various ways. Consciously grasping the world, coming to grips with it, centrally involves representing it.

Successful representation of the world is knowledge, which is intrinsically intentional. Knowledge is not something extraneous to consciousness in its intentionality but is what is aspired to in the act of cognitive intentionality. Representation is construed as knowledge when it is successful at representing the world, without remainder. In its success, knowledge marks an adequation between representation and object, a relation in which everything relevant (but not more) has been drawn into the depiction. By successfully bringing the world into presence, it becomes knowledge. The world has been comprehended. To come to grips with it successfully is to know the world, to have knowledge of it. Knowledge, as successful representation of the world, is to have control of the world because we have depictions without remainder. To have knowledge of the world is to have mastered it.

Paradoxically, the intentional engagement with the world is at the same time a withdrawal by the subject from that world. The paradox has to do with the role intentionality plays in maintaining and enhancing the subject's freedom by staying disengaged precisely because of the intentional relation. The act of representation is central to freedom. Representation is an act of drawing back from one's entanglement with reality, something that buffers the self from reality's restrictions and impediments. The idea of freedom here involves being able to maintain oneself in the context of a changing, complex, resistant world. This withdrawal is not just something peripheral to one's welfare as a being human. Instead, the ability to disentangle oneself from the world is what it means to be a human subject, an achievement of hypostasis. The freedom of the subject, autonomy, consists in disengaging the world enough to create a buffer for oneself. Freedom from the world, via withdrawal through the mediation of representations that grasp it, is central to knowledge of the world. Having knowledge is having autonomy.

This makes the curriculum representational at its core. In construing schooling as geared toward autonomy, representation plays a central role in the curriculum. A curriculum focused on autonomy has a representational foundation. A representationalist construal of the curriculum is what affords learning its aim of autonomy. It affords the idea that learning is about grasping and possessing knowledge. The curriculum interpreted as the knowledge aimed at in learning is an intermediary between the learner and the world. More to the point, in this model, it is through representation that the world is given to the autonomous subject. The thinking process of the student, as autonomous, is a form of possession of the world as given.

Representationalism is the traditional and still pervasive understanding in both the social imaginary and schooling. I do not deny its validity, but I question its privilege and completeness. I am skeptical of representationalism as the complete account of the knowing process. In particular, I do not believe it can stand alone. In what follows, I hope to "ruin" representationalism's privilege without totally rejecting the representational model.

To begin to unsettle the *privilege* given to the representational model we need to return to the fact that humans are embodied. Human embodiment involves a bodily center that is the core of thought, feeling, and action. This means giving a central role to the hypostatic, enjoying, worrying, bodily subject in it capacity as *knower* by uncovering bodily relations to the world that condition the act of cognition. Making bodily presence in the world central creates a conceptual opening for the recognizing of a relation more primary than the intentionality of cognitive consciousness. In a cognitive act, the metaphorical arrow that constitutes intentionality is directed toward the object of cognition. But that movement is itself part of the embodied nature of being human. These form, what for cognition are, unsuspected horizons or, in Levinas's words "the implicit—nonrepresented—horizons of incarnate existence" (Levinas, 1998e, p. 117). The unsuspected horizons are conditions that are the opposite of the disengaged freedom typically associated with conscious acts of representation. Whereas such acts of representation are construed as requiring a stance of independence from that which is represented, the implicit horizons of incarnate existence constitute a continued relation of dependency to the world. Cognitive intentionality hides as much as it reveals. In its explicitness, the act of representation forgets these implicit conditions. Nevertheless, for the explicit act of cognitive representation to be possible, it needs the support of the implicit horizons. This means that explicit representation is never pure or complete, but instead it is the cognitively visible tip of a much larger iceberg of incarnate existence. Although this doesn't negate representation, it does undermine its privilege and independence. It affirms an embodied engagement with the world that grounds the independence associated with cognition. Acts of representation occur in the implicit context of a pre-predicative world on which the incarnate subject is dependent. In particular, Levinas states,

"Earth and sky, hand and tool, body and other, condition knowledge and being in an a priori way" (Levinas, 1998e, pp. 119–120). These are not external limitations on acts of representation, but intrinsic conditions that make representing possible. In order to *be* representations at all they are conditioned by horizons that are themselves not products of cognitive intentionality. Without this bodiliness as tacit ground, representationalism remains incomplete as a model of knowledge, let alone the paradigm of knowing. In acts of cognition the subject is entangled in and dependent on the implicit horizons of earth and sky as well as hand and body.

By calling them forgotten horizons Levinas is drawing attention to the role of bodily sensibility in incarnate existence. Sensibility is a term that describes contact with something exterior which in not (yet) a cognitive object. The notion of sensible intuition includes an idea of exteriority which is not yet objective in character. This makes it different from the prototypical construal of vision in its objectification in the subject-object differentiation. More particularly, sensible intuition names a horizon that conditions such objectification. Sensibility doesn't merely fulfill thought, animating it so to speak, but comes before thought. Rather than merely making it an experience of an object, it is pre-objective; before the subject intends it through thought or perception, "the subject is steeped in it" (Levinas, 1998e, p. 124). The cognizer is immersed in implicit horizons, as tea leaves in hot water. This description undermines the urge to think of sensible intuitions as that which answers the anticipations of the cognitive intentionality. Levinas uses the term horizon to indicate this. Rather than an intentional projection by cognition, sensibility is a corporeal movement. This takes us prior to the cognitive intentionality of representation, prior to the control of a centered, cognitive subject in the act of cognition. Cognition is conditioned by the incarnated, the embodied, the corporeal.

The difference might be put in terms of open and enclosed experience. Embodied experience is first open rather than enclosed, whereas cognitive intentionality is enclosed because of its disengagement with the world via representations. Such enclosure makes invisible the implicit horizons which, though indispensable, are forgotten because of the way that cognitive intentionality represents. To uncover this open experience and its unsuspected horizons, we need to focus more directly on the structure of affect—broadly construed—in its relation to the world. Although there are many sorts of affective relations to the world, we can point to two contrasting ones. For example, the bodily affect of seeking novelty is related to the mysterious in the world while the bodily affect of nurture is related to that which is loved in the world (Panksepp, 1998). Each forms an incarnate relation to the world that does not involve cognitive representation. The relation of affectivity cannot be reduced to the mediation of cognitive representation. Whereas cognitive representation operates by means of a neutralizing mediating term—the representation—the incarnate relation of affectivity does not have this luxury, because the incarnate relation of affectivity is precisely entangled with the world. It cannot be indifferent.

The non-indifference of affectivity is central to the implicit bodily horizons for cognition. As such, it limits the scope of independence for cognitive intentionality. Conversely, viewing cognition as the primary way of engaging the world limits the scope of understanding human relations to world. From that angle, the lived bodily experience that grounds conscious intentionality is reduced to that which correlates with the intuitions needed to inform representations. Yet, there is much more to pre-cognitive bodily life than this, something that is missed when representational intentionality is construed as the primary relation to the world. When our models privilege cognition, it alters the felt awareness of concrete life by determining its sense through the neutralizing medium of representation. In sum, sensibility is a relation to the world that cannot be recuperated into the subject-object intentional structure.

Beyond representational knowledge

What I'm after in this chapter is a conception that unsettles the autonomy of the representational idea of knowledge as it is embedded in the curriculum. In the previous section I made explicit some of the implicit horizons that ground such knowledge. My aim in this section is to forge a conception that gives room for a knowledge relation with the world that takes us beyond cognitive intentionality. We can unsettle representationalism's primacy not only in terms of implicit bodily horizons, but also in its self-interest central to autonomy. Levinas often argues that our self-interest is not innocent. He laments that all violence starts with someone insisting "this is *my* place in the sun" (Levinas, 2001b, p. 53). This attitude appears in representational knowledge because the act of cognition makes the strange familiar, as if otherness is not entitled to a spot of the world. Representationalism's force of grasping reality is instrumental in maintaining our place of security in the world. Representational knowledge is used to enhance freedom—control not only over the non-human world but also over other humans. Knowledge as power includes gaining advantage over other people, either within society or within the family of nations. Knowledge as representation is thus entangled with questions of violence and peace, joy and misery, freedom and servitude, that is, with questions of flourishing marked by justice. Viewing knowledge as that which extends our power for domesticating the world puts into question the idea that representational knowledge is ethically neutral.

Representational knowledge, that which makes the strange familiar, is tied to conceptual abilities to reorganize the world in ways that further the subject's interests. Knowledge through which the subject domesticates its surroundings into a predictable, familiar, controlled environment is not about the way the world is outside of such control. Rather, it is a function of instrumental interests and egocentricity, something central to the mental operations producing such knowledge. Despite all legitimate safeguards and precautions that may have rightly been taken to eliminate idiosyncratic or emotional egocentric features, human self-interest remains central in this model. Such knowledge does not purely reflect the world as it really is but instead always represents it through the self-interest of manipulation and control.

To unsettle the primacy of the representational idea of knowledge, we need to uncover a deeper view of human subjectivity. In Chapter 3 we developed the idea that below the autonomous subject is a more primary subjectivity, namely, the responsible subject. That subjectivity is not defined by autonomy but by the responsible 'here I am,' the ego that forms in response to being called to responsibility. It comes through the vulnerability and exposure of the other that silently cries out: do me good. Responsibility doesn't require calculating its utility to show up. Instead, it appears as a deep subjectivity that recognizes the arbitrariness, if not violence, of claiming a spot in the sun exclusively as one's own. The arbitrariness of freedom shows up in the responsive character of this deeper subjectivity existing in the shadows of freedom's bright light. The call from the outside decenters the subject, bringing forward a felt responsibility impossible to elude. It stops the autonomous subject from living an easy egoism. It takes away the ego's peaceful consciousness of the world as a domestic home. A deeper subjectivity emerges in this appeal from the outside, one more personal than the autonomy of the *I think* and the *I can*.

When obligation reveals a subjectivity deeper and more personal than that of consciousness, a new awareness of the world emerges as well. Or, another experience of the world arouses a deeper subjectivity. Rather than a world that can be represented and controlled, the experience is of a world that calls. Rather than a potential extension of the familiar home that provides security for the independent subject, this is a world that calls to the subject from a permanent location outside of the orbit of control—truly external. Beyond representational knowing is an unsuspected relation to the world, one where the responsible subject is called to respect the otherness of the world, an otherness that is primordial and originary.

The call comes to the responsible subject *through* the familiar world of cognition from a time immemorial. It is not the familiar, known world that calls, but something beyond it. In the previous chapters I suggested that calls come to the teacher and inspirations to the student, each through the other. Here I use a similar schema to suggest calls and inspirations also come through the world, as other. Although Levinas himself only identifies the other with humans, I wish to extend his notion to a broader swath of reality, to include the world more generally (see also Benso, 2000; Joldersma, 2013a; Llewelyn, 2004). The world shrouded in a time immemorial or a time unforeseen functions as the other in a Levinasian sense. Although this is distinct from the human other, its otherness remains.

This has importance for our discussion of knowledge. When the world is other, it is outside of the encircling power of the cognitive intentionality of the autonomous subject. This means at least that the world is more than what we can grasp. Our representational accounts of the world are not entirely adequate, for there is a remainder outside our cognitive grip. The world is always more than our representations of it. Further, representations always bring with them human interests, putting the world within our encircling power of control. To name something *other* is to indicate something beyond the projection of meaning and interest constituting the represented object. The world as other makes room for it to be its own source of significance, rather than being a function of a representational scheme originating with the human subject (Joldersma, 2013a). It is to create the space for the world to indicate its own meaning.

The issue here concerns the possibility of relating to the world in a way that it reveals traces of its own signification. It is the possibility of hearing the world issuing a call, showing itself as something that has an intrinsic significance rather than merely a function of human representation. The world that calls has "a surplus of significance," showing a "glory that challenges and commands me" (Levinas, 1998b, p. 131). Levinas uses the term *glory* to indicate this excess. The significance outside of cognition is an intrinsic glory that challenges the adequacy of human representation of the world. Glory always escapes our representation. But is there a way to indicate that sort of relation with the world, without reducing it to an intentional representation? Is there a way to have a relation with the world that allows it to disclose its glory in a non-representational way, as something that challenges and unsettles human representation?

The metaphor of vision is often used to describe the cognitive intentional relation to the world. It makes sense to say that when we develop a representation *of* something we are depicting the world *as* that thing, which is a visual metaphor of projecting meaning onto the world. Using the auditory metaphor of listening in relating to the world changes this. Chapter 2 introduced the term *listening* in the learner's relation to the teacher as other. Here I employ that metaphor to reveal a deeper relation to the world. In the listening metaphor the subject is passive with respect to the world. First, one cannot help but listen to what is incoming; unlike vision, one cannot avert one's ears. And second, to listen is to be open to what is incoming, to be open to something external. The metaphor of listening reveals an inescapable openness to possible signification from a source outside of one's own interests and control. In listening, one is forced to be open to meaning that comes from outside of one's conceptual scheme. The listening metaphor reverses the intentional arrow. In vision, the arrow is from the subject to the world, whereas in listening, the arrow is incoming, from the world to the subject.

I'm using the metaphor of listening to indicate something pre-representational that, nevertheless, is a relation to the world. The pre-representational character is important in order that the world itself can break through with its own signification. If reality is significant beyond what the subject attributes to it, then the relation to that reality must go beyond the representational scheme brought to it by the cognizing subject. I'm using the metaphor of listening to designate one such pre-representational mode. A call cannot be brought to mind because the response is always later than the call, for it comes from a time immemorial. The call is not present in the mind as a representation. The trope 'immemorial' indicates resistance to being brought into presence, into memory as a representation. The mode of listening is diachronic: there is a time lag between what is heard and the call, as if listening is always belated. This ensures the call's pre-representational character. More particularly, the glory that shows itself in the call is intrinsic to the external world precisely because it challenges and commands the subject to be a responsible listener. The listening metaphor uncovers a relation to the world in which it remains outside of our human representational grasp.

The two metaphors, visual and auditory, are not incompatible. I am not replacing vision with listening. Instead, listening conditions vision. The visual metaphor gives pride of place to the sovereignty of autonomy. In the vision metaphor, the independent agency of the subject takes center stage, and thus the independence of representation and its imposition of meaning on the world. However, when we situate this in the auditory metaphor, then the active is situated in the context of the passive, autonomy in the context of responsibility. The world calls forth to the responsible subject, providing an implicit horizon for the visible through which the world appears to cognition. The audible world situates the visible world. Unrepresentable glory conditions the claims of visionary representation. The cognitively projected meanings already find themselves placed within a signifying glory not of their own making.

But the auditory metaphor, though important, is only one way of indicating how we can unsettle representational knowledge. There is a second sensory metaphor I want to use, that of touch. Earlier I characterized representational knowledge in terms of the hand's grasp. In this mode, representational knowledge is modeled as grasping reality, metaphorically bringing it under the hand's control. But there is more to touch than merely grasping. Although grasping does involve a kind of touch, not all touch is grasping. There are ways of touching that are beyond the grasp (Joldersma, 2005).

In the ordinary sense of touching something, it is a proximate relation, describable with the word *contact*—there is no distance between the two. The visual metaphor suggests independence, a distance between the one who sees and that which is seen. There is little confusion between the seer and the seen. By contrast, the touch metaphor closes this distance. The distinction between the toucher and the touched is inherently ambiguous: contact means that to touch is also to be touched (Merleau-Ponty, 1962). The touch metaphor reveals an ambiguous passivity.

We can apply this to the hand's action. Grasping is one particular way of touching. Grasping is a touch that minimizes one side of a touch's ambiguity, namely, the passivity of being touched, while maximizing the activity of touching. Literally, the hand grasps by isolating something from its surroundings and holding onto it with opposable thumb and fingers. By forming a container which isolates, the grasp diminishes the passivity of being touched (the incoming arrow) and augments the act of touching (the outgoing intentional arrow). Cognitive acts of comprehending are metaphorical acts of grasping. Concepts are often construed as containers, that is, categories into which something fits, thereby isolating it from its surroundings. As a result, we touch the world through the grasping activity of concept formation. And so, metaphorically the act of comprehending the world through concepts minimizes the passivity of the incoming arrow of being touched and maximizing the outgoing arrow of touching. The arrow of representing—of imposing significance based on the subject's conceptualizing process—is a form of touching without being touched.

There is more to touch than grasping. There are many tactile situations in which the grasp is minimized. Levinas gives the example of an open hand that caresses, which he characterizes as a touch that does not grasp (Levinas, 1969, p. 157). Here the hand does not form a container that isolates. Instead, a caress is a light touch that does not seek to control or incorporate what it touches into an isolated, familiar world. Rather, it is a touch that allows what is touched to remain free, outside of the control of the hand. A caress does not isolate the touched from its surroundings, restrict its freedom of movement, or force it into a particular shape or size. In a caress the touch minimizes its active grasping side by allowing the touched to be itself: the caress is tactful in its touch. This emphasizes the passivity of touch, letting that which is touched to reveal itself without the active control of the grasp. Levinas says, "What the caress seeks is not situated in a perspective and in the light of the graspable" (Levinas, 1969, p. 158). This sort of contact I will call a 'tactful touch.' A tactful touch does not grasp, but is situated in the ambiguity of activity and passivity. A tactful touch allows the world to reveal itself outside of the signification imposed by grasping it. The tactful touch is a contact the world prior to cognitive representation.

A tactful touch is contact with the world toward a time unforeseeable. Levinas uses this temporal metaphor when he says, "the caress consists in seizing upon nothing, in soliciting what ceaselessly escapes its form towards a future never enough, in soliciting what slips away as though it were not yet ..." (Levinas, 1969, p. 157). The metaphor of tactful touch is inherently temporal, indicating a relation toward the world in a future never yet present. The phrase "time unforeseeable" designates temporally the world beyond representation: not present to the hand, not available to vision, but always still in the future. The tactful touch is too early, a contact that comes before we know what to expect, before we grasp what we are touching. The trope *too early* protects the contact from eliding into cognition. The tactful touch reveals something coming to us from a time unforeseeable.

The tactful touch metaphor uncovers a relationship with the world that is a 'letting be.' This relation leaves unresolved the ambiguity of passivity and activity, connecting to the otherness of the world without domesticating it, to the strangeness of the world without making it familiar. It reveals the world in its enduring enigma from the perspective of grasping. Grasping makes the world clear, certain, rational, factual whereas the tactful touch leaves it be, allowing it to disclose itself in its otherness. Tactfully touching is way of contacting the world as a mystery that inspires, a way of connecting before cognition represents it. In the tactful touch the unexpected can show itself without being domesticated in representational knowledge. Tactful touch reveals the excess of the world beyond our expectations, beyond cognitive mastery. It is touching the unforeseeable that connects to inspiration. A tactful touch is an avenue to hope.

I develop the two metaphors—listening and touch—to construe how we contact the world prior to cognition. The auditory mode elicits the temporal metaphor of time immemorial while the tactile mode employs the temporal metaphor of time unforeseeable. The temporal modes indicate pre-representational relations with the world in which human subjects are primarily passive. That passivity allows the world to disclose itself to the subject.

This sort of disclosure also reveals a kind of truth. A representational view of knowledge has traditionally identified truth with being in a position to judge whether or not the representation adequately depicted the world. Truth in that construal is a function of the representation itself, where the subject is in a position to judge how well the representation corresponds with the world as represented. Rather than discarding this view of truth, I believe an adequate construal of truth should be expanded to include the non-representational relations of listening and touch.

The idea of truth that fits well the relations of listening and touch—that comes along with the call heard by the responsible subject and the hope that comes to the inspired subject—is, to borrow a phrase from Lambert Zuidervaart, "truth as life-giving disclosure" (Zuidervaart, 2004, p. 77). On this view, truth involves the idea that the world reveals itself as itself. The responsible (auditory) and inspired (tactile) subject exists for the sake of truth. One *hears* the truth, through one's responsibility that allows the call to be heard. Responsibility allows the world's truth to be given to the subject. And, in the second metaphor, the inspired subject exists for the sake of truth. Inspiration is the susceptibility that allows truth to intrude human subjectivity. One *touches* the truth, through one's inspiration via the tactful touch. Truth, in these senses, involves the world showing itself as itself. Truth is the self-givenness of the world, a self-disclosure of the world to the responsible and inspired subject. The world can disclose itself by being enigmatically available. The temporality of time immemorial (auditory) and time unforeseen (touch) blocks the privilege of the time of the present (vision) and its central cognitive self-interest of control.

The responsible subject can hear the call of the world in many ways. But centrally, the call to justice is a self-disclosure of the world to the responsible subject, where truth is the world's self-disclosure that leads to human flourishing. Zuidervaart states, "by 'life-giving' I mean a process in which human beings and other creatures come to flourish, and not just some human beings or certain creatures, but all of them in their interconnections" (Zuidervaart, 2004, p. 97). Life-giving disclosure means the way that the world calls the responsible subject to respond. These responses include practices that promote social justice, enhance greater economic equality and encourage more sustainable use of resources. These practices recognize the intrinsic glory of the human and non-human worlds. Ultimately, for Zuidervaart, what makes it true disclosure is that it leads to "life-promoting and life-sustaining fidelity to principles …" (Zuidervaart, 2004, p. 100). I interpret idea of principle here to be the revelation of the world as itself through hearing and tactful touch. The passivity of these modes leaves the responsible and inspired subject open to life-disclosing truth.

This somewhat lengthy excursion into the idea of knowledge, ending with an all too brief discussion of truth, is meant to enrich our understanding of the 'what' of the curriculum. A representational view of knowledge, with its built-in human interests, is not the extent of the curriculum. The knowledge constituting control over the world, which is a powerful interest of freedom and autonomy, needs to be supplemented by the modes of listening to and tactfully touching reality, by being responsible for and inspired by the world. Interested knowledge is relativized by touching and hearing the world in a way that lets it be itself. When the world breaks through with its call and inspiration, in its glory, it reveals itself as life-giving avenues for human flourishing. By indicating a different relationship to the world, we are able to relativize the grip of the representational model of knowledge that is central to many if not all of the disciplines that presently constitute the curriculum. By construing the *content* of teaching and learning in this expanded way, we can more clearly hear and feel that such content uncovers the world's call and inspiration.

Calling and inspiration in the curriculum

The courses that typically comprise a curriculum are not arbitrary aggregates of knowledge. Instead, they are organized along particular fields of study called subjects. Especially secondary and post-secondary institutions follow this pattern, dividing the curriculum into the recognizable disciplines. Although there are clearly variations among the arts, humanities, social sciences, and the natural sciences, they are typically construed as bodies of representational knowledge—specialized areas of knowledge that give a grip on reality. However, when we use the metaphors of listening and touch, we can enlarge what counts as disciplinary, and thus what should be included in the curriculum. Although viewing disciplines as ways to grasp the world remains, what counts as disciplinary should include pre-representational relations with the world, which in the previous section I marked with the ideas of listening and the tactful touch. This connects the curriculum directly to the ethical.

Earlier chapters developed two ethical orientations: the learner's inspiration by the teacher and the teacher's responsibility for the student. The curriculum, too, offers an ethical orientation. It is through the curriculum that we encounter a third relation to the other, this time to the world. In the first ethical relation, the teacher is outside the expectations of the students, disturbing their preconceptions through inspiration. In the second relation, the student is outside the purview of the teacher, calling the teacher to responsibility. But teaching and learning are more than just general relationships marked by ethically charged responsibility and inspiration, for they always involve learning or teaching *something*. In these ethical relationships the curriculum marks for both teacher and student the responsibility to and inspiration by the world as other.

The world as *other* is not the body of knowledge characterized as representational. The knowledge we associate with disciplinary content doesn't get us to the otherness of the world. The world shows itself as other through the various disciplines of the curriculum, which become portals for listening to and touching the world. This means at least two things. First, it means that teachers are not merely conveyors of settled information, but act as trustees of listening to and tactfully touching the world. And, second, it means that students do not merely learn content but are inducted into becoming attentive to the call and inspiration of the world, to listening to and tactfully touching the world.

The call from the world creates a kind of responsibility that can be called *trusteeship*. Teachers, especially in secondary and tertiary education, are typically named by the various disciplines: biology teacher, English instructor, professor of history. This is often interpreted to mean that such a person is an expert in a disciplinary body of knowledge—biology, English literature, history. An expert is someone who has learned the contours of the discipline and perhaps contributes new representational knowledge. But the disciplinary names teachers give themselves indicate something more, namely, being a *trustee*. A trustee is someone who is entrusted with a responsibility. The teacher as trustee is not merely responsible for a body of representational knowledge, such as the content of the discipline of biology. Rather, being a trustee also reflects something deeper, in two ways. First, it means remaining open to hearing a call from the world as other—a call to responsibility. But a discipline is also a concrete location of inspiration of unexpected possibility that comes via the tactful touch. Being a trustee is thus, second, being open to that inspiration. Being a trustee is to feel that the discipline's current understanding of an area of reality is a historically situated present response to the world's self-disclosing. Being a trustee is being aware that such self-disclosure ultimately always comes from beyond present representations, requiring continuing attunement to new ways the world might reveal itself. It means recognizing that the world's call and inspiration come from beyond the world as represented. To be a disciplinary trustee is to be called and inspired by the world as other, to recognize the ultimate disciplinary relation to the world through the call beyond representation and the tactful touch beyond the grasp.

The teacher's relationship to the world, embodied in the curriculum, makes clearer the student's relationship to the teacher. Earlier I argued that to be a learner is to be inspired by the teacher as other. However, we can now locate a more distant node of inspiration, one coming from the world via the curriculum. This is not a mere addition alongside the teacher, but comes through his or her trusteeship. The teacher as other does not merely disturb the student in an abstract fashion, but such disturbances come through the teacher via the curriculum from the world as other. The world as other comes concretely through the teacher via the curriculum as disturbances in the expectations of the student.

We can also look at this from the perspective of the teacher. The teacher is called to responsibility not only by the presence of the student as other, but also by the call of the world as it continues to disclose itself. The teacher's responsibility to the student is not only directly to the student per se, but also comes via listening to the call of the world in its disclosure over which he or she is trustee. The encounter with the student that calls the teacher to responsibility includes pulling the student toward understanding of the world as represented by the disciplinary knowledge of which the teacher is a trustee. As such, faithful explanations and exercises to induct the student into the discipline's representational knowledge is part of doing the student good. But this knowledge is itself conditioned by the call of the world as other. Doing the student good thus includes re-orienting the students to become attuned to the call of the world beyond disciplinary representations. The disturbances that undoubtedly occupy teaching are themselves framed by the trusteeship constituted by listening to the world through one's discipline. One does one's student good by helping them listen to how the world discloses in its call to responsibility.

Construing curricular subjects as concrete locations where the world discloses itself beyond representations expands the way schooling can view the curriculum. Typically, subjects are viewed as disciplinary bodies of knowledge. Further, these have traditionally been construed as encyclopedic, where each discipline represents a rationally constituted body of knowledge, including clear boundaries from other disciplines.

Together the disciplines are construed as constituting an integral, unitary whole, thought to mirror the coherence of the world itself. The latter was thought to have a particular geography composed of definable areas bounded by conceptual borders and composed of patterns accessible through cognitive intentionality. On this construal, reality's natural borders configure the disciplinary boundaries as well as their content, something mirrored by cognition in the curriculum's representational knowledge. Together this encyclopedia then constitutes a coherent package of accurate knowledge about the reality. This view remains embedded in the model of the curriculum in today's high schools, colleges, and universities, where the entire panorama of disciplinary knowledge is an integrated entity forming the backdrop for the subjects that constitute the curriculum. Thus fields of study such as mathematics, physics, biology, psychology, accounting, physical education, art, and English are viewed as various elements of a coherent rational whole.

I am not totally rejecting the unity of the curriculum as an encyclopedia. However, this idea needs to be disturbed and contextualized. The metaphors of the auditory beyond vision and the tactful touch beyond the grasp disturb the convergent gathering forces of the encyclopedic interests of the unified curriculum. Although I am not completely in favor of chaos, neither am I convinced that total integrality is an adequate understanding of the curriculum. A central reason for my suspicion comes from Levinas. He characterizes such unity as a totality (Levinas, 1969). According to Levinas, the history of Western thought "can be interpreted as an attempt at a universal synthesis, a reduction of all experience...to a totality wherein consciousness embraces the world, leaving nothing other outside itself, and thus becomes absolute thought" (Levinas, 1985, p. 75). The unity of the curriculum, on this reading, is an artifact of the totalizing move of thought. On this construal, its unified character is a function of a reduction of experience by the cognitive intentionality to a unity of representations.

Someone might object that the integrality of the curriculum merely mirrors a unified picture of the world rather than the reduction of experience to concepts. There is some merit to that objection. It makes some sense to think that reality itself is not incoherent, that it doesn't have contradictions embedded within it. Yet Levinas's insight goes beyond this. The problem with the reduction of experience to a unified system of thought is that it leaves nothing outside itself as an intentional structure. A unified world picture doesn't just grasp the world through a conscious set of justified beliefs, but has become absolute, leaving nothing outside the integrating totality of that vision. Western thought generally has involved the desire to reduce reality to a rationally grasped system. This desire is grounded in the self-interest of human power and sovereignty over others and the world. The emphasis on unity and integrality in defending a disciplinary curriculum is ultimately grounded in the human self-interest of grasping and control. The cognitively derived unity of the curriculum reflects human self-interests.

Conventional criticisms of the curriculum in terms of the unity of abstract theoretical knowledge are often done to make room for a more practical idea of knowledge. Practical knowledge is then heralded as involving more directly job-related expertise and skills. This criticism has become louder in the neo-liberal shift of schooling for the global economy (Spring, 2008). This criticism has some merit. There is no doubt a need for the practical knowledge of the professions and blue-collar laborers. In fact, all students could benefit from such practical knowledge, not just those who might enter such occupations. However, the idea of practical knowledge remains within the grasping metaphor, having to do with control. Practical knowledge continues to involve schemas originating in the subject as autonomous in order to initiate particular actions in the world. It is still a matter of coping with the world through control. As such, this knowledge is no closer to passively listening to the world or tactfully touching reality in order to let it disclose itself. Rather, it remains a version of cognitive intentionality. Practical knowledge doesn't get us beyond the representational model of knowing, to the idea of the truth as life-giving disclosure. It does not yet get us to the passivity that I'm associating with call and inspiration.

My argument is that reality includes something beyond the reach of representationalism's integrating coherence. Our reach for the unity of knowledge is, at least, partially a reflection of a human totalizing interest imposing itself on the world to effect control for some self-interest. The metaphors of tactful touch and of listening give the potential for contact with the world in its self-revelation that unsettles current conceptions of curriculum unity. Although my idea of tactful touch and listening is not meant to abolish integrality, it is meant to unsettle the possible hegemonic effects of the encyclopedic unity on which we base the curriculum of formal schooling. The non-visual metaphors unsettle the totalizing grasp of the disciplines as bodies of representations.

This allows us to think about the curriculum in a more complex way. Tactful touch's unsettling work implies a looser fit of the disciplines within the picture of the curriculum. Disciplines such as the natural sciences, social sciences, humanities, and the fine arts are not merely bodies of representational knowledge; they can also be viewed as so many different possible places for listening to and tactfully touching the world. Conceptually this means that the categories in the curricular canon are more than mere boundaries reflecting a rational division of labor and reality, but as so many ways of listening to and tactfully touching the world. Each subject in the curriculum can be construed as a differently tuned antenna that creates channels for listening for something beyond the settled content, and as so many different ways of tactfully touching. Reality has enough plenum to allow for these kinds of attunement.

One might argue that attentive listening and tactful touching can occur without disturbing to totalizing work of a unified curriculum, that these supplements do not disturb the curriculum's unified structure. However, supplements always uncover a lack; in their supplementing they also supplant. Enlarging our construal of disciplinary spaces unsettles the curriculum's encyclopedic claims. It reveals more clearly that the traditional encyclopedia is *reductive* because it shows that there is more to disciplines than rationally organized cognitive intentionality and a division of labor. Moreover, what is added to the disciplines are not more representations. Rather, the additions are partial, multiple ways of listening to and touching the world. But this also means that we are listening to and touching multiple worlds—differences that defy integration. The plurality of the plenum accessed through the disciplines remains wild, resistant to the unity of thought. The various fragments function as something beyond what we expect in the unity of the encyclopedia. In listening for something of which we are not sure, in tactfully touching something beyond the grasp, we relativize the categories of the curriculum, indicating that our representation of reality is always only partial. The openness of each discipline to reality's self-disclosure draws attention to the fact that encyclopedic unity too quickly and too confidently reduces reality to overarching representations. The openness brought by the metaphors of listening and tactfully touching depicts a deflationary move, one of going beyond the view of disciplines as bodies of knowledge.

I am arguing for a less-unified view of the curriculum, suggesting that a teacher's trusteeship implicitly reflects the recognition that each discipline is a concrete node of listening to and touching the rich plenum of the world, without prior commitment to its possible unity or integrality. This leaves more room for experiencing reality as *other*, that which calls concretely from beyond our expectations and that which inspires us to new possibilities. Curricular subjects are concrete avenues for the world's self-disclosure. The call and inspiration from somewhere transcendent disturbs the cognitively inflected curriculum directly, not only via teachers and students. The curriculum, as a structure within formal schooling, is also a site where a non-representational truth emerges, experienced as the truth of life-giving disclosure. The responsible and inspired subject hears and feels the truth. A teacher's responsibility allows the world's call to be offered, through the curriculum, to the student as other. And the inspired student exists for the sake of truth which comes through the curriculum, via the teacher as other. Inspiration is the susceptibility of the student to the teacher as other that allows truth to intrude into the student's subjectivity. A student touches the truth through his or her inspiration. Truth is the world showing itself as itself via the curriculum as organized by the teacher. As self-givenness, the self-disclosure of the world to the responsible and inspired subject comes from beyond representational knowledge.

The inspired student might hear the call of the world in multiple ways, differently in different classes, without an overarching principle to explicitly bring them under a unified set of representations. The truth of the world's self-disclosure constitutes so many traces of (human) flourishing. Without knowing the particularities of what might lead to such flourishing, the curriculum calls and inspires the student to work toward actions "in which human beings and other creatures come to flourish, and not just some human beings or certain creatures, but all of them in their interconnections" (Zuidervaart, 2004, p. 97). These responses may be practices and actions that promote peace and justice, greater economic equality, and more sustainable use of resources. They involve actions that respond to the glory of the non-human world. If inspiration and calling reveal the world as itself through listening and tactful touching, then the curriculum is the portal for the inspired student to respond positively to its possible life-disclosing truth.

Linking the curriculum to call and inspiration re-situates the way that something transcendent unsettles the more usual conceptions of the curriculum. The ideas of listening and tactful touching give us a way to think about how a call from a time immemorial and an inspiration from a time unforeseen unsettle our traditional view of knowledge. This call and inspiration contextualizes the claims of representational knowledge by exploring their implicit transcendent conditions. Ultimately, such unsettling comes from the other. Although *the other* means many things, it refers, at least, to those who have little voice in society and around the globe, the marginalized, the vulnerable, the poor. At present, the current disciplinary divisions effectively help maintain our focus on the abstract, representational knowledge of the pure sciences, fine arts, and humanities, something that helps keep at bay our consciousness of social issues. What I'm arguing for is a view of the curriculum that unsettles this view. It suggests construing curricular subjects as something more, transcending our self-interests of grasping and controlling the world. What I'm after is a way to loosen the curriculum in such a way that it becomes a location where ethical disturbances might enter. In addition to the two asymmetries I identified earlier as the student-to-teacher and teacher-to-student relations, the curriculum itself is also a location for call and inspiration. Not just as an addition to the representational knowledge that constitutes the curriculum, but as a disturbance of that knowledge from within. What gathers the curriculum is not first its cognitively derived unity, but its role as so many portals of ethical call and hope. What provides its coherence is not rational unity but the multiple ways that the world calls us to responsibility and inspires us to hope.

5
Institutions

Abstract: *This chapter addresses the institutional character of education. Here a Levinasian framework reveals that institutionalization is both a limitation on, and a concretization of, positively valorized educational experiences. In particular the analysis shows that formal organization is an important avenue for discharging its ethical obligations in a responsible manner while simultaneously imposing restrictions on such possibilities. Because of the way that organization of educational practices occurs, ethics and justice as regulative conditions turn out to have a disruptive character. This alternative perspective reveals that while formal schooling is irreplaceable as a way to respond to the ethical call to responsibility, orienting action toward justice, it is also continually disrupted in that response by the same conditions that make it possible.*

Keywords: institutionalization; social justice; social responsibility

Joldersma, Clarence W. *A Levinasian Ethics for Education's Commonplaces: Between Calling and Inspiration.* New York: Palgrave Macmillan, 2014. DOI: 10.1057/9781137415493.0009.

In this chapter, I connect the first three commonplaces to a fourth one. When we recognize that learning, teaching, and the curriculum are each conditioned by calling and inspiration, we can reinterpret their place in their formal milieu, institutions. Although Schwab uses the term *milieu* as the last commonplace, I will restrict the discussion to institutions, examining both their limitations on and space for ethically oriented education. On the one hand, institutionalization is an important avenue for ethical responsibility and inspiration while, on the other hand, it imposes restrictions on those ethical orientations. Because of the way organization occurs, ethics and justice, as regulative conditions, are disruptive of institutions. While formal schooling at its best is our society's way of educationally responding to the ethical call to responsibility and inspiration to hope, simultaneously it requires continual disruption for an ethical orientation to the justice of life-giving disclosure to remain educational.

I will center my analysis of institutions around the radical responsibility to, and inspiration by, the other. But in this chapter I will also develop more systematically Levinas's conception of justice—ethical responsibility as it appears in social roles, structures, and relationships. My main aim is to connect Levinas's notion of justice to the organizational and institutional character of formal schooling. The role of justice is to interrupt existing institutional dynamics by infusing ethical responsibility into social roles and organizational structures. Justice may disrupt many of the formal features of schooling, including high-stakes standardized testing, the standards movement in curriculum, normalization via grading, and hierarchical supervision and power. The idea of justice will reveal that institutionalized schooling has two sides: one which opens to opportunities for justice and one which erects roadblocks for education animated by justice.

Formal schooling is typically institutionalized as organizations with stable patterns of practice, including internal economies, administrations, social roles, supervision, budgets, and bureaucracies. Institutionalization is at once a boon and a bane, an opportunity and a danger, an opening and a limitation. Education occurs within the tension of these inherent tensions of institutional life.

The limits of institutionalization

Although I will argue in the next section that institutionalizing learning, teaching, and the curriculum in formal schooling is a function of deliberations that attempt to answer responsibly the call of justice, it is, nevertheless, also true that such institutionalization has particular liabilities on the possibility of education. In this section I hope to show that ethical orientations disrupt the quieting, if not conserving, character of institutions as organizational structures. An institution's inner economy and bureaucracy can be viewed as structures that limit the call and inspiration of ethical transcendence. Institutionalized schooling is not totally friendly to the student as other, the teacher as other, or the world as other.

In Chapter 3 I argued that in teaching the call of responsibility comes through the student as other. A teacher feels obligated to that particular student, regardless of the others in the class. Even after a teacher has spent a great deal of time explaining the lesson to that student, if he or she still does not understand, the felt responsibility remains, although a teacher might choose to ignore it. The feeling of obligation is never discharged.

This felt responsibility shows up in institutionalized schooling as tensions in teaching practices. A teacher might feel he or she hasn't developed clear enough illustration for important content. A student drops by with a problem that seems very urgent just when a teacher has scheduled time for class preparation. Although a teacher is behind in the curriculum's content, a persistent student keeps asking for further explanations during the class period, using up valuable instructional minutes. An administrative budget decision fills someone's classes with 40 diverse learners, making it very difficult to test, let alone get to know, them in any meaningful way. In grading a test, a teacher feels as if a particular student has been in an entirely different course. These various examples show tensions in the various tasks associated with teaching.

We can rightly interpret these tensions as a clash between the institutional schooling and the teacher's felt ethical responsibility to the student as other. Take, for example, the pace of a class. The structure of formal schooling is, in part, a sorting and selecting process in which students with comparable abilities are grouped together. The institutional character means that the administrative process places only those students in a class who qualify for the curriculum offered there, using certain general criteria to choose only students who have certain similarities, including the right prerequisites and adequate cognitive abilities. For such schooling to be successful, it requires a certain sameness among the students, including background knowledge, pace of learning, ability to write papers and tests, industriousness and self-discipline. So, the students are carefully chosen even before they show up in a particular class. This ought to mean that the teacher can safely pace his or her class to ensure they get through their curricular content while leaving no student behind.

But any teacher knows it is not that simple. The planned pace often is undermined by something more immediate, namely, a student who doesn't seem to quite understand. When a particular student asks a question for clarification, a teacher feels obligated to *that* student, regardless of how long it might take and who else is in the class. The tension between the predetermined pace of class and the immediacy of the student's question is a tension between the way that schooling is institutionalized and the particularity of the call to responsibility that comes through that particular student.

Institutionalized teaching is unsettled by the ethical call to be responsible to the student, to do good to *each* student who walks into class. This shows most clearly when the student seems out of place academically, not learning as fast or as easily as expected, or when he or she reads poorly and has difficulty grasping the concepts so clearly presented in class. The call to "do me good," coming through the student as other, felt as continuing responsibility to that student, precisely becomes a tension because the pace of the class has been set by the institutional machinery. The ethical obligation disturbs the smoothness of the institutional practices. A teacher cannot choose to not be responsible to a student as other despite the predetermined pace of a class curriculum. Yet, the class must go on.

The tension of the institutionalized class pace can be construed in a fundamental ambiguity about the identity of the student. This is a tension between the student as a singular, irreplaceable being and the student as a replaceable, universal learner. It is a tension between, on the one hand, formal schooling assuming more-or-less identical students in the class that keep up with a certain pace of teaching, and on the other hand, the felt responsibility to (any) one particular student as other, irreplaceably singular. This is a tension between a call originating from beyond the institutional criteria and the criteria of sameness that constitutes the implicit institutional contract of the class. The call of responsibility shows up as the uneasy feeling that *this* student is not expendable, that he or she cannot be neglected or abandoned. Keeping a particular pace, despite careful institutional procedures, shows institutional limitations on the call to responsibility that comes through the student as other.

A second tension can be revealed by turning more directly to the curriculum. Established bodies of knowledge have been institutionalized as the content of the curriculum in schools. Institutionalization of the curriculum is typically shaped by the disciplinary matrix in which such content is embedded. Disciplinary content is also structured by administrative units such as credits, courses, diplomas, certificates, degrees, and programs. Although they can be construed as opportunities, these administrative units are also designed to limit learning. They function to create endings. Without credits, courses, and diplomas there would be no end to what would be felt as important for the student to know. As requirements for students to accomplish, they also create closure on what would otherwise be an infinite set of obligations for teachers and schools. They are institutionalized limits that allow for discharging otherwise limitless responsibilities. Without the clarity of the finite requirements embodied in such institutionalized structures, teachers would remain obligated to the students in their charge indefinitely.

Semester-length courses at the undergraduate level provide a good illustration of this. Typically divided into three contact hours over the span of about 14 weeks, this structure provides limits to the teacher's call to responsibility that would otherwise be open-ended, in two ways. On the one hand, without the limit of three hours per week, there would be no boundary on the teacher's responsibility to do the student good in terms of daily teaching time. And without the 14 week semester span, there would be no end to the teacher's obligation to continue to instruct that student indefinitely. The structures of organization are institutionalized ways of coping with the powerful call to responsibility that face teachers in relation to their students.

These are no doubt very good limitations. Yet they are felt as tensions. First, it is felt as a tension within curricular content. There is a seemingly infinite amount of content that is not yet presented when a lecture-hour, or semester course, or degree program comes to a close. There is always more disciplinary content than can be fit into the finite time slots that schools allot for teaching. This excess is felt by the teacher as trustee of the disciplinary content: leaving out material betrays the disciplinary matrix. The students haven't learned all they should have. Second, it is felt in the tension between the lack of mastery of the material by many students and the evaluation schema that say they have successfully navigated the courses in the program in which they are graduating. Their grasp on the material falls short of the teacher's knowledge as trustee of the disciplinary content, something that is the responsibility of the teacher to orchestrate. The teacher's call to responsibility as disciplinary trustee is betrayed by student who doesn't have a deep enough grasp of the material for which he or she is now officially deemed to have competency. The institutionalization—that is, the limitation of a disciplinary body of knowledge within a school setting—shows up as tensions between the call to responsibility as infinite and the structures that discharge this responsibility as finite.

Another tension arises in the institutionalization of the teaching, between content and pedagogy. The curriculum is institutionalized as explicit representations that constitute a discipline's current body of knowledge. Being loyal to the explicit representations of disciplinary knowledge in the curriculum is felt as a limit on how a teacher might present this knowledge in class. In order to make things clear, a teacher simplifies and translates, straying from the discipline's accepted and standard representation of knowledge. But in reaching students with understandable language teacher may feel they are betraying their trusteeship of that disciplinary knowledge. The disciplinary knowledge is experienced as limiting the sorts of explanations, metaphors, models, and exercises teachers might responsibly employ in their teaching, yet responsibility to the student demands it.

The call to responsibility that arises from the encounter with the student unsettles the explicit, standard representations of disciplinary content. The presence of students in a teacher's classes intrudes on the stability of the standard disciplinary articulation of knowledge. Students seem to undermine the stability of a course's content by their very presence. But not in their identity as institutionalized alter egos, as rational autonomous subjects. Instead, it is the student as other that disrupts the institutionalized curriculum. The student as other might spontaneously disrupt the deliberately planned explanations that faithfully articulate disciplinary content. The teacher feels the responsibility to draw on *other* metaphors and analogies, new examples and illustrations, different concepts and ideas in order to meet the demand for clarity from the interrupting student as other. The right thing to do *pedagogically*, in the teaching situation, is to supplement if not supplant the discipline's standard explanation or representation with others, ones that might even betray the fidelity and purity of the institutionalized knowledge. The call to responsibility demand by the student to 'do me good' unsettles the institutionalized disciplinary content. Settled representations of this knowledge are an institutionalized limitation on the call to responsibility that orients teaching. The otherwise infinite call to responsibility, coming as a felt obligation to re-engage the course content in a new way in order to do a student good, is limited by the standardized representations of disciplinary knowledge.

A final example of how institutionalization limits the call to responsibility: All schools have as part of a teacher's task the chore of assessing their students—grading quizzes, tests, examinations, papers. The institutionalization of teaching includes assessment of how well each student has mastered curricular material. Teachers often lament that grading is not easy or pleasant. This institutionalized practice is an implicit social contract between teacher and students in which teachers expect the majority of their students to successfully master the material if they put in a reasonable amount of effort, given that they show up for classes reasonably often and have been placed properly in the class. Teachers design tests, papers, and exams in ways that most students can pass and at least a few will achieve top grades. Perhaps more to the point, teachers conscientiously grade in a way that treats everyone fairly and does justice to the implicit or explicit standards of disciplinary knowledge. These are all functions of institutionalized practice.

Yet there is a felt tension in grading. Institutionally, grading limits the ethical responsibility of the teacher to the student. This shows itself in several ways. First, grading can be seen as a way of bringing to a close the otherwise unending responsibility of a teacher to a student. Final grades, most clearly, do not constitute formative pedagogical feedback, from which a student is meant to learn. Conversely, if formal assessments were meant primarily as pedagogical feedback, they would not need standardized gradations; effective feedback is more nuanced and individualized than letters or numbers can indicate. Instead, grades are final judgments, namely, ones that put closure to the learning process. To assign a grade is to say, in effect, the course is done, the unit is over, here's the relative level of achievement. Or, to say the same thing: here's the judgment, my pedagogical responsibility is discharged. In other words, grades are institutionalized structures designed to bring closure to an otherwise indefinite obligation to the student. This is in tension with the felt pedagogical responsibility to do the student good as a learner.

Second, institutional limitation shows up in the process of grading itself. Central to grading is a judgment of each paper or exam. These are decisions about whether or not that particular student has learned this material in a satisfactory manner. While grading the teacher meets face-to-face each student, individually and inescapably. But in this act, the teacher meets the student in two ways, one as an institutionalized rationally interchangeable identity, and the other as someone interrupting that institutionalized context, namely, the student as other. The teacher meets the student institutionally as a cognitive knower, a rational subject who has learned the material as presented in the course. In this sense, each student is construed as a cognitive alter ego, the same as all the others in the class. They are all comparable. From an institutional perspective students are commensurable, rational knowers who have equal opportunity and skills to learn a body of knowledge. In terms of their institutional identity, students are replaceable, cognitive, rational subjects. Despite idiosyncratic or biographical differences, as institutional students are completely comparable. It is to the students as interchangeable cognizers that a teacher feels justified assigning grades based on their work.

However, the grading teacher meets the student in a second way, below the first, as someone who interrupts the institutionalized sameness. This is the student as other. Grading also always inescapably shows that there is no way to student-proof the teaching process. For example, a teacher might ask crystal-clear questions in an exam or frame his or her expectations on a paper with amazing clarity. Yet, in grading the teacher finds out that the student has spontaneously interpreted those words differently, answering questions a teacher did not ask and writing papers that the teacher did not specify. Grading brings into focus that each student seems to learn something a little different from what the teacher teaches. This experience indicates that in grading a teacher encounters a student in a second way, as an *other* that does not fit well into comparison schemes required for institutionalized grading. The unexpected misunderstandings a teacher encounters in grading point to meeting the student as other.

In the call to responsibility of the student as other, the teacher's well-drawn methods of institutionalized grading get disrupted by an unsettling ethical undercurrent. In grading, the institutionalized methods and content are disquieted by the student as other that calls 'do *me* good in particular.' The obligation to *that* student, as a singular other rather than a token of an institutionalized universal category, is what undermines the ease of making judgments in grading. The student as unique unravels the process, showing the limits of cognitively inflected comparison. Whereas grading requires students to be interchangeable and comparable, the student as singular marks something incommensurable and irreplaceable. Grading relies on the student to be comparable with others while feeling the disquiet of the student as a singularity that cannot be compared. The irreplaceability of a student as other ruptures the ease of assessing the student, of comparing similar alter egos. As a result, a teacher is forced to make subjective decisions rather than come to rational conclusions about assigning a grade to a paper, an exam, a course.

Precisely because of the infinite obligation that comes with the asymmetry of the teacher's relation to the student, the institutionalization of grading is a way to limit such responsibility. The process of institutionalizing grading means that teachers limit the responsibility through treating students as commensurable. It is the comparability of students that makes grading a finite chore, a task with an end, one that makes possible the decisions of assigning points to questions and letters to papers. Without institutionalization, the incomparability of the students, namely, each student as a unique other, a singular being, would make conventional grading impossible.

In general, we can say that institutionalization creates limits on the felt responsibility of teachers. Although I will not elaborate here, I would suggest that this also goes for the relationship of students to teachers. The institutionalization of teachers means that their function as infinite sources of inspiration for the student is limited. As institutionalized, the unsettling character of such inspiration is limited both by the comparability with other teachers and by the ending of courses, semesters, and programs. Institutionalization is a way to limit the call and inspiration as it shows up in the processes of teaching and learning.

From ethics to justice

In the previous section I showed the limits of institutions on calling and inspiration. However, the lens of ethics can also reveal them as places of justice. Although Levinas is known more for a conception of ethics, he does have a notion of justice, and it functions as a way to think about society, including its structures and institutions. Justice for Levinas is more than merely a relation between two people—a two-some isolated from the rest of humanity. Justice comes into play when someone is in relationship with more than one person simultaneously, namely, always. When we approach this through the first-person perspective of a subject in relationship with a second person, the other, there are also always others in relationship with the subject, which can be thought of as third parties. Levinas develops his idea of justice via what he calls "the third."

According to Levinas, "The third party looks at me in the eyes of the Other" (Levinas, 1969, p. 213). He is saying that already in the dyad of the subject and the other, the subject is also aware of others, third parties. This means that the ethical call to responsibility arising in the encounter with the other also somehow already involves third parties. They too are *others*, and can be called in a slightly odd phrase, *other others*. This means that in any encounter with an other, the call "do me good" is not limited to *that* other, but is also already felt as coming from beyond the immediate other, from the other others, the third parties. The ethical call to responsibility spills outward to become a network of social responsibilities rather than merely an individual relation. The inevitable multiplication of the ethical call is for Levinas the terrain of justice. Justice involves an original multiplicity of the dyadic ethical call to responsibility.

But this is not merely a multiplication of the dyadic call. In isolation, being called by the other means an *unending* obligation to *that* person. However, the presence of the third party changes this. In Levinas's words, "Human multiplicity does not allow the *I*—let us say it does not allow *me*—to forget the *third party* who pulls me away from the proximity of the other" (Levinas, 1998b, p. 195). The subject is pulled away from the responsibility to the immediate other, but not because of self-interest or because the responsibility is discharged. Rather, the presence of third persons interrupts the *infinite* character of someone's responsibility to the immediate other. The other others *also* call to the subject "do me good." The responsibility that is multiplied with the implicit presence of multiple others is also divided because of their presence. Each relationship of infinite responsibility is interrupted by the call to responsibility coming from the other others. The interruptions show the social character of each ethical relationship, and together they form a web of relations. The subject's concrete ethical relation to one neighbor is actually part of a social web of ethical obligations, each interrupting the others. And the subject is obligated to sort this out.

There is a further complication of this social web. Levinas writes, "The third party is other than the neighbour, but also another neighbour, and also a neighbour to the other, and not just his counterpart" (Levinas, 1999, p. 142). To unpack this, let us start with the subject's relation to the other, the neighbor. The third party is not only another neighbor for the first *subject*, although he or she is that. That third party is also an *other* for the subject' immediate other ("a neighbor to the other"). This means that although the immediate other calls the subject to responsibility, the third party calls the subject's immediate other to responsibility. Thus the multiplicity of responsibilities is not merely for the first subject (from its first-person perspective) but forms a web of ethical obligations between all the others. The presence of third parties certainly complicates the picture. In other words, the actual network that constitutes any social fabric is a network of dyadic ethical obligations. It is here that justice emerges for Levinas.

But again, justice is not merely the multiplication of dyadic ethical obligations formed by calls that come through and to multiple others. Rather it emerges from a transformation of the ethical relation itself. In an imagined single dyad, bracketing the other others, the extent of responsibility to the other is clear—it is *unending*, to *that* other. There is no question about it. But when one considers the same ethical relation complicated by calls from the other others, the unending nature of the responsibility of any and all of them is called into question. The presence of third parties disturbs all those responsibilities. Levinas asks, "What am I to do? What have they already done to one another? Which comes before the other in my responsibility? What are they, then, the other and the third party, in relation to one another? Birth of the question" (Levinas, 1999, p. 142). The presence of third parties not only disturbs my singular responsibility, but it also gives rise to something more—questioning. That is, it gives rise to stepping back and reflecting on what to do. It gives rise to asking questions, inquiries into how best to discharge one's responsibility to the many neighbors, given that others are also already discharging responsibilities to that person and the fact that I have responsibilities to others as well. It means being deliberate about asking what others are doing for each other, what still needs to be done, who best to do it. It means prioritizing the concrete actions that might begin to discharge one's obligation, calculating what would be most effective, and so on. The presence of the third party, in other words, leads to conscious thought, rational deliberation, communication, collaboration, and practical action.

It is this development that gives rise to justice. To be *just*, the subject must be busy comparing and making judgments about how to discharge equitably the many calls to responsibility. As singular, each other is unique, irreplaceable. As unique, each of the others is impossible to compare. The subject cannot easily compare and prioritize the various responsibilities to tidily discharge them in the best order. Yet, Levinas offers, "There must be a justice among incomparable ones. There must then be a comparison between incomparables and a synopsis, a togetherness and contemporaneousness.... It is this disinterestedness, when, as a responsibility for the other, it is also a responsibility for the third party, the justice that compares, assembles, conceives, the synchrony of being and peace, take form" (Levinas, 1998d, p. 16). Because of the presence of the many others that constitute the network of society, we have a call of *justice* and not merely an ethical call to responsibility. Justice involves comparing the incomparable responsibilities to each of the others, all of whom are rightly incomparable, but which require comparison, nevertheless. Justice involves the call to make judgments about how to move forward in this difficult, if not impossible, task.

The consciousness and thought involved in justice do not mean that each *other* now is reduced to being an alter ego of all the other others, ultimately similar to each other and the subject. Justice does not negate the otherness of the others. Levinas again, "The love of one's fellowman, and his original right, as unique and incomparable, for which I am answerable, tend of their own accord to make appeal to a Reason capable of comparing incomparables, a wisdom of love.... Here the right of the unique, the original right of man, calls for judgment and, hence, objectivity, objectification, thematization, synthesis" (Levinas, 1998b, p. 195). It is loving my neighbor that requires the judgments constituting justice. Comparing incomparables grows from one's love of the singular other because that other also is in relation with others who are also one's neighbors. What the call of justice uncovers is a form of deliberate judgment that is different from the self-interested cognitive intentionality of mastery and control. Here the intentional judgments have as their outward-directed arrow the objective of justice, developing justice out of the multiple responsibilities to the other and the other others. Not making these judgments is a failure of my first-person ethical responsibility. The subject's responsibility to the other is not only to be obligated to that other alone but is also to ask about the other others. Justice is action and thought based on the web of social relations founded in ethical responsibility.

Justice in institutions

Institutions such as schools are obvious places of multiple relationships of ethical responsibilities. Within a classroom, a teacher is in multiple relationships. When a teacher encounters one of her students as other, implicit in that relationship are all the other others sitting in the rest of the desks. It would be not be just for a teacher to attend only to the call of that one student and neglect the rest, the other others in the class. As an other, *each* student rightly demands a teacher's responsibility. The teacher must, despite the call to infinite responsibility by any one student as other, justly limit responsibility to any one student on the basis of other students who are equally worthy of a teacher's responsibility. Therefore comparisons must be made. But each student is unique, irreplaceable, making such comparisons impossible. Yet the incomparable students must be taken as comparable, for the sake of responsibility to each, precisely because of the call of justice.

The teacher's comparison of incomparables is done so that justice might prevail. It would be unjust if one student got more attention than the others just because he or she was first—or merely nearer, or louder, or more persistent, or more obnoxious, or better looking, or the same race, or the right gender. Justice says *each* of the other students has an intrinsic worth, even when they came later—or are soft-spoken, or polite, or self-effacing, or unattractive, or a different race. But equally, justice is the recognition that observable markers such as these are not the basis on which to give attention—they are not the markers of obligation. The ethical orientation of responsibility out of which the call of justice emerges comes from beyond any of these recognizable traits, from beyond one's consciousness, from the singular uniqueness of each student as other. The call of justice thus also emerges from somewhere transcendent, beyond the pale of recognition. Each other is unique—irreplaceable—not just the one that faces me most directly and obviously. Justice therefore demands limiting responsibility to any one for the sake of the others who also are irreplaceable.

Institutionalized schooling is one concrete site for positive responses to the call of justice. In this way, institutions function in an overtly ethical way, as sites for justice. As such, schools open up ethical spaces by distributing indefinite responsibilities among the students in an equitable manner. Institutions legitimate the limitation of a teacher's infinite responsibility to any one particular student because of responsibilities to the other students that are gathered together. Institutions are openings for justice. This gives a positive perspective on institutionalization—the relative legitimacy of institutionalized practices and procedures. Organizational strategies and regulations can be thought in terms of justice. Some of the ways that institutions operate must be seen as a way of distributing a divided responsibility among incomparables—justice.

Let's return to the previous example about a teacher's decision concerning how fast to pace a class. The decisions that are made in this regard are connected to the student as other, whose very presence calls: 'do me good in particular.' But in the ethical relationship with that one student as other is always already the presence of third parties—the other students in the class. This raises to the level of *question* the responsibility of pacing the class. It requires deliberate thought and judgment. Decisions of how fast to pace the class can now be characterized as calculations based on comparing incomparables. Precisely because there are other others in the class, also calling out 'do me good,' we can construe the pace of the class as a possible location of justice. If the teacher adjusts the pace entirely so one particular student will be able to understand completely, this is not fair for the rest of the students. Although clearly a call to responsibility comes through the questions of the one student who obviously does not understand, to ignore entirely the rest of the class would be a matter of injustice. But, on the other hand, ignoring that one student entirely is equally unjust. And so, the pace of the class comes about through a comparison of incomparables, for the sake of justice within the classroom.

This can also be seen with respect to the curriculum. The curriculum's standard, explicit disciplinary representation comes from the scholars who through the years developed that knowledge-base. Yet, to teach is to feel the call to responsibility through a student's ability to understand. A teacher's urge to restate the lesson in new metaphors and simpler models is an attempt to be a responsible teacher. However, in doing so it is possible to betray the discipline's accurate representations, one agreed upon by a community of scholars. Further, previously I argued that disciplines do not merely represent a settled and closed representational content, but are means to attest to something beyond, to the way that reality might be disclosing itself. Although teachers might implicitly maintain that disciplinary knowledge is primarily about grasping reality for the sake of control, and that explicit representation of such knowledge is based primarily on agreement of the community of scholars within particular disciplines, nevertheless, teachers as trustees also are responsible for going beyond such expressions of control, to give testimony to the possible ways reality might show itself if we let it be. Reality's disclosure calls for a teacher's trusteeship, obligating a teacher to remain faithful to a particular understanding while simultaneously listening to the call and tactfully touching beyond the grasp. And it is this nexus that creates limits to the responsibility of a teacher to heed the call that comes from a student's inability to understand, that is, the call to responsibility as a teacher. And so, the teacher as trustee must compare incomparables, namely, the call to be faithful to reality's disclosure, the settled understandings of disciplinary experts, and the call to do the students good by helping them understand. These are not always easily harmonized. And so, we can construe the institutionalization of disciplinary knowledge in the curriculum to be a set of limits on the infinite demands for new explanations to students, for the sake of doing justice to reality's disclosure.

More generally, at its best, institutionalization can be viewed as a set of limits that creates particular space for the call of justice. Although there are many reasons for institutionalization, not all of them are positive or legitimate; at its best we can think of institutionalization as a process of attempting to address issues of justice. Given the call to responsibility that resonates in the many relationships found in schools, institutionalization at its best can rightly be construed as so many attempts to compare the many incomparables in order to create a proper configuration of responses to such a multitude of calls, one that might do justice to all the competing calls to responsibility. When such a configuration congeals into stable structures and practices, roles and regulations, we have institutionalized those many practices, creating a stable nexus over time, in response to the call of justice. That is, at their best, we can think of educational institutions as standing attempts to respond justly to the many infinite obligations that are associated with education.

The many limits can also be interpreted as creating space for other responsibilities. For example, the parameters we call programs, divided into semesters and constituted by a finite number of courses, can be construed as limits that allow current students to finish so that others may start the learning process at that particular institution. Or, in higher education, we can think of office hours as limits on responsibilities to students precisely so that teachers can also discharge other responsibilities, as scholars, researchers, faculty governors, and community service providers. Thus the fact that office hours limit responsibility in one area is not only a limitation of a particular responsibility, but simultaneously the creation of space for possibly discharging other ones. The category 'office hours' can be viewed as the institutionalization of a practice that, at its best, thoughtfully balances the simultaneous pulls of incomparable obligations. Moreover, deliberatively achieved balances become stable configurations, replete with names and stylized practices. These might include, in formal schooling, familiar terms such as semester hours, schedules, programs, certificates, and degrees. And collectively, this set of stable configurations can be called institutionalized schooling, collective responses to the call of justice.

Two things must be pointed out, however. First, these stable configurations are sets of deliberate judgments about *incomparables*. Just because they are compared—indeed they have to be compared—does not mean that they are *actually* comparable, without a disquieting remainder. This means, at least, that the judgments made in the institutionalization process always are less justifiable than their seeming finality might otherwise indicate. As a result, an inherent arbitrariness runs as an inextricable subaltern current through institutions, even at their very best. The shadowy presence of such currents means that, despite our best deliberative intentions, our decisions fall short of the various responsibilities that we are attempting to balance. This just doesn't disappear when a decision is made to limit one to make room for another obligation, equally infinite in character and equally limited by the deliberative process itself. The incomparability of the various calls to responsibility means that any achieved balance is always rightly contestable. Justice is never quite achieved through such a balance although it may well be best attained in that way. Even at their best, institutions are thus always somewhat precarious in their very ethical structure, a less than solid array of decisions to enact the call of justice.

This means, second, that institutionalized limitations don't disappear even when it can be pointed out that they are enacted for the sake of justice. The singularizing function of each ethical obligation doesn't disappear when deliberations happen in response to other others. That is because this singularization goes in two directions. First, it points back to me: *I* am obligated. The call to responsibility is the feeling that there is no such thing as a substitute, that it is *my* responsibility to ensure the unique other will not be harmed. Just as the good Samaritan was not able to look over his shoulder and gesture to the wounded man, "there is someone else coming who will take care of you, I'm going to be late for my meeting in Jericho" so also the call that conditions responsibility is the feeling that I am not able to gesture over my shoulder with the message that there's a substitute coming who will discharge my responsibility to the other, justifying my limiting move. The ethical relation runs deep, below the level of intentional consciousness, at a level where I feel the infinite responsibility as mine, inescapably. In the other direction, singularization shows up in the feeling of obligation to *that* other. It involves the implicit experience of that particular other as irreplaceable. It is the intuition that I cannot merely substitute another other for the one that faces me now; no, *this* particular student calls to me, incomparably and irreplaceably singular. The presence of other students, which require deliberative limitation, does not expunge this singularity. Instead, it shows up as a genuine tension in the context of, say, a class of 25 students. This is evidence of the subterranean call to responsibility that reaches from below the institutional level of schooling, even when such institutionalization is precisely in response to the other others which also call me to responsibility. No responsible response to the call of justice is totally just.

Educating for justice

The idea of justice is not merely inward-looking, forming and unsettling institutionalized schooling. The call of justice unsettles the idea that schooling exists merely for maintaining the status quo, for slotting future workers into an economic world order, or for giving advantage to some while excluding others. Schooling today is situated in a problematic status quo, an increasingly oppressive globalized economy, and a growing set of inequalities. This is schooling in the globalized twenty-first century. The call of justice makes us aware of these features of our present temporal location. This is crucial for education to emerge in schooling. Education intrinsically involves normativity and hope, being called to look outward, to society and culture, and inspired to action—political, economic, environmental, social. The call of justice orients schooling's commonplaces, so that education might emerge.

Social philosopher Hannah Arendt locates education between past and future. She suggests that the gap between past and future is a "region of the spirit...paved by thinking...into which the trains of thought, of remembrance and anticipation, save from whatever they touch from the ruin of historical and biographical time" (Arendt, 1968, p. 13). This gap for Arendt signals a set of antagonistic forces, a past that presses us forward and a future that drives us back, into which humans are inserted in the present. Humans in the present battle both the past and the future to create space in the present. More strongly, humans are the site of the clash between the past and the future—to be human is, in a sense, "making a stand against past and future" (Arendt, 1968, p. 11). That stand is what gives us our present existence, splitting the continuum of time.

Certainly, Arendt is right to suggest that because schooling is situated in time, it is located between past and future. One way to gloss this is to acknowledge that formal schooling is partly an enculturation process where the next generation is inducted into the knowledge, skills, and attitudes held dear by the previous generation and its collective culture (including its disciplinary knowledge). This move discriminately preserves a collective, objectified remembrance, saving from the ruin of time what would otherwise disappear. This is the forward push of the past into the present via education. And, simultaneously, it seems right to suggest that formal schooling is partly a process in which the next generation is invited to rethink how things could be better and different. What else is this but having the future intrude into the present, in the form of collective anticipation, giving opportunity for a future that pushes against the continuity of the past? So institutionalized schooling can rightly be thought as located in the present, which is that time between remembrance and anticipation, between past and future.

In fact, this could be stated more strongly. Without anticipation, schooling might become purely a conserving enterprise which merely socializes students to accept an established narrative as the inevitable context for the present. And without remembrance, schooling might lose its particular moorings and waft on any wind of change. For teachers the present situation rightly makes little sense without the past or the future, without situating education between remembrance and anticipation, memory and vision. Teachers teach effectively precisely because they self-consciously locate themselves in representations of the past. It is because they know society's memories that a new generation can make particular sense of the present. And it also means, we might say, that teachers self-consciously locate themselves in anticipations. Teachers teach also by self-consciously locating themselves in representations of the future. Also because they embody society's visions, a new generation can make better sense of the present.

But for schooling to be called education, it should not be content to merely be situated between memory and vision. Education emerges from the orientations situated in the transcendent conditions of a time immemorial and a time unforeseen. Education is a location where goodness is funneled into the world through answers of gratitude as its participants orient their actions outward, into the world. That is, education emerges in the positive responses to the call to obligation and the inspiration to hope. Education assumes an outward orientation in such positive responses. Education contributes to the larger society's good, emerging in schooling's positive responses to transcendence, ethically oriented by a time immemorial and a time unforeseen.

The call, which shows up as obligation, orients the outward-directedness of schooling beyond the institution's walls. The call forms a transcendent condition that orients organizing classes, gathering students, developing curricula, doing research. More particularly, I'm suggesting that the condition for education is a calling that comes from outside the school, awakening in schooling a responsibility for the good of society via the marginal, vulnerable, poor, destitute, weak, voiceless members of society. I'm arguing that education occurs in formal schooling through its structural conditioning, in its obligation toward the public good of society. Education does not emerge when schooling is oriented to the advantages of some students over others or even to merely passing on disciplinary knowledge. Education emerges when schooling's commonplaces are oriented to being responsible to and for those in the world around us who cannot advocate for themselves, a responsibility to and for the world. And thus, in the ultimate sense, the conditioning call for *education* steers schooling away from other possible primary goals, such as academic excellence, personal development, finding truth, or the American dream. Instead, it is to embody institutionally an answer of gratitude in terms of obligation to the other. It is to see the institution's educational enterprise as a gift to the globalizing world in the twenty-first century.

In addition to grounding outward-directed responsibility, transcendence also grounds education's outward-directedness via an inspiration for hope. The impulses for teaching, learning, research, and service are forms of hope that are not easily discouraged. Such hope inspires teachers to work with difficult students—and students to persevere with poor teachers. Such hope motivates educators to tackle difficult topics—and administrators to do thankless tasks for ungrateful staff. All inspired by the real possibility of doing something worthwhile in ways they have no business to expect. Moreover, the hope that grounds education is implicitly directed outward, in the same direction as felt obligation: to the others in society, outside of school. Perhaps it might lead to a brashness of action, to attempt impossible things. Hope, as something felt within while outward-directed, makes small, seemingly insignificant efforts part of a permanent change for good. Hope makes local actions successful parts of global tasks. In short, hope pulls formal schooling to become education by orienting it outward, to action toward the other others, those in the world outside the classroom.

Understanding education as founded on these conditions accomplishes three things. First, it invites institutionalized schooling to see its very structure in terms of the good of others. More specifically, understanding education as conditioned by an enigmatic call to responsibility and an equally enigmatic inspiration to hope suggests that teaching is not for the sake of the participants, or to maintain the purity of disciplinary knowledge, or to establish an alternative culture, or to return to a bygone era, or to keep the next generation from straying from the fold, or to help certain individuals get credentials so that only a small segment of the population might flourish. No, education, conditioned by hope, is a gift—to society, to the world, to the globe. As a gift, it is something given without seeking return. No-one gives a gift with an eye to getting something back; instead, what makes it a gift is precisely that it does not come back, exchanged full value, paid back in its entirety, let alone returned unopened. This invites us to see education as an offering not only to one's own society but to the entire world. Education conditioned by a call to responsibility means that its community is there for the world and not the reverse, and that the task of its community is to work for inclusive flourishing, here and now. Education is other-directed, including specifically to areas outside of the communities that support and sponsor it, that pay for it, that have worked long and hard and have sacrificed much to establish these institutions. To say that education is conditioned in this manner is to view its work as gifts given for the sake of human and global flourishing. To view education this way is to suggest that structurally it is not inward-looking, but it contributes to the public welfare of society and effects change for common good across society and the entire globe.

Although formal schooling is a specialized institution within modern society, its call to responsibility comes mostly through the vulnerable and weak in our society, through the troubled and threatened ecosystems and biomes around the globe. Institutionalized schooling is undergoing increasing pressure to be reduced and distorted to serve a country's ability to compete in a global economy, thus increasingly asked to focus on individual learning by students whose own reasons for gaining credentials is to get a subsidized ticket to a prosperous life. Yet to be educated, schooling is obligated by something quite different. The stutter of time immemorial comes most clearly through those in our society who are marginalized, silenced, suffering, wounded. Institutions responding affirmatively to that call see their mission centrally in terms of working for the public good of those who are the most vulnerable and the ecosystems that are the most threatened. Rather than seeing schooling as a set of opportunities for individuals to achieve a set of credentials or to acquire skills that will help select individuals do better financially, education is the affirmation of the call to responsibility. Education emerges in the felt responsibility to encourage society's younger members to engage in effective collective actions for public good, especially for those who have little or no voice. To educate then is to respond, as educational institutions, by being outward-directed.

Interpreting education in this way implies that schools themselves can become actual pockets of hope. Hope is the expectation for something better when we have no business believing that there is any chance of it becoming better. Schools enacting education can become pockets of hope within society; their work can involve expecting the impossible to happen, and preparing students for the impossible. This means to prepare students to consider idea that things can be different, better, despite the perceived trajectories of social forces and political landscapes, and that they can make a difference. Moreover, to be inspired to hope also means that such schools manifest, in their very structures and regulations, similar openness, risk, and vulnerability, conditioned by a future unforeseen. That is the educational character of schooling's structure. Of course, this doesn't mean that actual schools are not on the whole conservative places, structures whose design is to maintain the status quo and resist change. Instead, it means that despite such conservatism, for a school to be educational means its conserving structures are disrupted and cannot remain merely conservative, for otherwise it ceases to be educational. This can be seen in the struggle of schools to embrace those who are different, who don't fit so easily the 'mold' of the supporting community, or who are different from the majority of the students, whether that be because of religion, race, gender, language, class, or sexual orientation. It can be seen in the struggle to make day-to-day operations more sustainable, with a lighter ecological footprint, despite the increased cost. Embodying hope means schools show evidence of impossible flourishing that its participants—teachers, students, administration, operations, community—expect to come, soon. To be pockets of hope is to recognize that what makes us human is not our autonomy and freedom, but our being inspired and responsible. What makes us human at its deepest is our heteronomy. To be hopeful is to be non-indifferent to the sufferings of those around. To educate is to raise awareness in our students and ourselves of the felt inspiration of a time unforeseen. To educate means that hope seeps into the very fabric of the school, into its everyday commonplaces, evidence that to be an educational institution is to be an organization of hope.

Formal schooling as education is structurally conditioned to be oriented toward the good of society. Schooling conditioned by obligation and inspiration involves being called to educate a generation to struggle toward bringing human flourishing in our communities, our societies, around the globe. It involves being inspired to educate for the purpose of raising a new generation of active people who see themselves as responsible for being a healing hand in society, concretely, for the marginalized, the oppressed, the silenced, the outcast, the poor within our midst. It is called to see itself as instilling in a new generation the need for environmental action before it is too late. Education, conditioned by a call and a hope, is obligated and inspired to make a genuine and important contribution to society as a whole, to the public good if not planetary well-being.

The relationships that constitute human flourishing are intimately associated with social roles, institutions, societal structures and dynamics. Thus the thought and action that respond to the call of justice—comparing incomparables for the sake of justice—shows up in the social roles, institutions, and social structures that encourage human flourishing. The call of responsibility and the inspiration to hope show their traces especially in social places where society's members, especially those who had little voice, now have a fuller membership and a more secure place. It shows up in places where people begin to enact ways of living within the limits of the finite earth which is the inevitable, if not often neglected, context for human flourishing. As such, transcendence is a call to social action anchored in actualizing human flourishing in the context of sustainability.

That need for thought and action comes to us here and now in the context of a society that is filled with pain, suffering, woundedness. It is precisely in the cries and tears of suffering—the hunger of those who are without food, the struggle of those for whom there are no jobs, the pain of the abandoned in refugee camps, the poverty of inner-city squalor, the ailments caused by industrial pollution, the danger to those ostracized by their communities, the destruction of a civil world, the danger of sweatshop working conditions, the increasing gap between rich and poor, the gays and lesbians shunned by our communities—where call and inspiration show up. These concrete locations call out for justice, obligating education to work toward bringing human flourishing in our communities, societies, around the globe. The ethical orientations of call and inspiration find their concrete locations as the call of justice. Education emerges when school's participants cannot just fold their arms and remain aloof, indifferent to the plight of those around us. To act justly is to struggle to help those who suffer and who have no voice of their own. Struggling for justice means working to honor everybody's rights, to develop an ethical community where no-one needs to hide in fear of judgment and oppression. Education ethically oriented to the public good is obligated and animated by the call of justice.

Conclusion

Abstract: *The book concludes with a short chapter that brings together the ethical orientations of the commonplaces developed in previous chapters. The conclusion explains how the commonplaces interact for education to emerge, and reiterates that it emerges most fully when schooling's everyday activities do not stay within the walls of school. Rather, education breaks out when schools respond positively to being called to responsibility for the world's vulnerable and to being inspired to hope that things can get better. Education emerges when schooling's ethical orientation is ultimately animated by the call of justice that comes from the world.*

Keywords: education; ethics; justice; Levinas

Joldersma, Clarence W. *A Levinasian Ethics for Education's Commonplaces: Between Calling and Inspiration.* New York: Palgrave Macmillan, 2014. DOI: 10.1057/9781137415493.0010.

Conclusion

Formal schooling has been drifting away from education. It has been increasingly dominated over the past decades by non-educational interests, including corporate profiteering through high-stakes testing, developing human capital for a globalizing economy, and domesticating compliance through a surveillance bureaucracy. These interests threaten the education that ought to occur in formal schooling.

My intent has been to reorient the commonplaces of schooling to allow education to show through. Learning, teaching, curriculum, and the institutional setting need to be more explicitly situated within a set of ethical conditions. Education emerges from this ethical orientation. I have been using ethics to indicate an original condition that constitutes a person's non-totalizing relation with the other, which I have developed via two felt ethical experiences, calling and inspiration. Each of the commonplaces is grounded ethically in these experiences, and this marks them as educational. The commonplaces become educational in the context of an ethical call to responsibility and an inspiration to hope, which directs them ultimately toward human and other creaturely flourishing. When formal schooling responds appropriately to the ethical, it will have the goal of individual and collective human flourishing, something marked by social justice. It is this ethical orientation that turns formal schooling toward education. I am arguing for two claims. On the one hand, to be educational is to be animated by twin ethical orientations while, on the other hand, to be educational is ultimately to respond to the call of justice. I'd like to briefly restate each of these in turn.

My argument in the book is that education's commonplaces are conditioned by two temporal undercurrents, a time immemorial and a time unforeseeable. These give rise to two disruptive affects, a felt call to responsibility and a felt inspiration to hope. Education emerges in the dynamics of these twin affects. In the day-to-day activities of formal schooling, education is an emergent phenomenon, arising from the dynamic interplay between being called to normative responsibility and being inspired to hopeful action. Each of the commonplaces has a different role to play in this emergence. Learning is first ethically oriented by being inspired to welcome the disturbances coming from the teacher as other, while teaching is first ethically oriented by the felt responsibility for the student as other to do the student good. Formally, each of these is an asymmetric relation, different from the other. The two are not mere reversals of each other, and they are not each half of a reciprocal relation. Rather, it is the unique ethical orientation of each that keeps them asymmetrical. Yet, both are needed for education to emerge in the everyday activities of schooling.

But education's emergence is more complicated. Both teaching and learning require a *double* asymmetry. Teaching is not only ethically oriented by the call to responsibility that comes from the student as other, but it also is inspired by the hope for justice that comes from the other others in the world. Teaching as an *educational* activity emerges in the dynamics between the call to responsibility from the student and the inspiration to hope that comes from the world. Likewise, learning is not only ethically oriented by the inspiration to welcome the disturbances that come through the teacher as other, but it is also called to responsibility by the other others in the world. Learning as an *educational* activity emerges in the dynamic between the inspiration to hope coming through the teacher and the call to responsibility coming from the world. But this does not make teaching and learning the same; they have fundamentally different dynamics—the relation to the immediate other is different, as is the relation to the other others. Both sets of dynamics are required for education to emerge in the context of formal schooling.

But the third commonplace also figures into the complexity. Without an ethical orientation embedded in the curriculum, education would still not completely emerge. In particular, teaching would not be completely educational if it is only oriented by the call to responsibility from the student and by the inspiration to hope for justice in the world. And learning would not be completely educational if it is only oriented by the inspiration to welcome disturbances by the teacher and by the call to responsibility for doing justice in the world. The educational nature of both learning and teaching also requires an ethical orientation through the curriculum to the world. Disciplines are revealed as places for listening to and tactfully touching reality. The auditory relation of listening to the world is the ethical orientation of relating to the world so that it reveals traces of its own signification. And the tactile relation of tactfully touching designates how world reveals itself outside of the signification imposed by grasping.

The learner is not merely disturbed by the teacher as other, but unsettling also comes via the curriculum from the world as other. And the teacher is not merely responsible to the student as other, but is also ethically oriented by the call from the world that continues to disclose itself, over which he or she is a trustee. Central to the teacher's responsibility to the student is orienting him or her to be attuned to the call of the world and to be inspired by the unexpected possibilities that come via a tactful touch. The world as heard and touched enters the classroom through the teacher via the ethical orientations of the curriculum. Each curricular subject then becomes an antenna through which a student can listen for something particular beyond its expectations, and can tactfully touch the world. The ethical orientation of the curriculum emerges in the dynamic between listening and tactful touch, between calling and inspiration. Education emerges when the ethical orientations conditioning teaching and learning intertwine with that of the curriculum.

But teaching, learning, and the curriculum remain commonplaces inside the walls of schools. For education to completely show itself, schooling's ethical orientations ultimately need to point beyond the institution and be oriented toward the world. Concretely the normative calling and inspiration through which education emerges inside the school also animates education toward justice outside of the institution. Justice emerges in the ethical call that comes through all the other others in society; it involves the affective disruptions that arise through the vulnerability and fragility of others in the world. In today's society, these are the undocumented workers, the homeless, environmental refugees, war victims, gays and lesbians, the uninsured, and the unemployed. These are actual members at the margins of societies who are suffering and oppressed, but they can symbolically and forcefully represent all the other others that give education's affective disruptions an orientation outward, outside of the school walls. Education ultimately emerges when the commonplaces respond to the call of justice from outside the classroom, coming through the concrete suffering of those who actually have little or no voice in the world and through the vulnerability of the environment that sustains life. When this seeps into schooling's commonplaces—an obligation to the concretely vulnerable, those who are victims, in our society and around the globe—then education emerges most completely.

Education thus involves a collective obligation for which we never sign a contract, for which there is no written plan to limit involvement to a reasonable level—say with every other weekend off, a three-week summer vacation, and eight-hour, day-time shifts. From the perspective of the persons who feel this obligation, it appears as something that is unending and larger than can be fulfilled—something that makes the phrase *a time immemorial* appropriate. Those involved in formal schooling might say: If only we had been there to negotiate the educational obligation when it first arose, then we could have written into the agreement a *limited* responsibility. But by the time obligation disrupts it is already too late. The call that comes through the vulnerable is an obligation that comes before students, teachers, and administrators are ready. There is no time to adjust it more to their liking—it comes from beyond their grasp, out of reach of their domesticating memory, their representing ability that controls. Their passivity before the call turns out to be their concrete responsibility to the refugee, the homeless, the poor, the voiceless, the illegal aliens of the world. Their concrete responsibility to the suffering is evidence of a deeper subjectivity, namely, a responsible being. It creates the subjectivity of being responsible for the vulnerable in the world. Being responsible is something that comes from obedient responses to the call that comes before being ready to respond.

Equally, education also thus involves inspirations to hope that are animated by the world outside of school. Such inspiration doesn't just come from anywhere, like a bolt out of the blue, from some ethereal sphere. Instead, it comes concretely, through the other others. In particular, much like the call to responsibility, this also comes concretely through the presence of vulnerability, destituteness, misery, pain, suffering. The other others that inspire are strangers: unregistered immigrants, the poor, the homeless, the social outcasts. To be inspired is to be interrupted by these concrete others, inspired to action by their suffering and vulnerability. The subjectivity of hope involves not being able to evade being affected, not being able to resist the very personal effect of being hopeful in acting on the suffering and pain of others, their oppression and marginalization. Education intrinsically involves inspiration to hope arising from the world.

The hope that arises in the world transforms into action. Ultimately, education's worldly hope involves its participants being moved to action in society and around the globe. The positive response to inspiration is a non-indifference to the pain and suffering of those around it. Education's hope is embodied in the inability of its participants to be non-indifferent to the plight of those around it. Its hope shows in the joy and delight of working toward the real possibilities of human flourishing. Hope, the conviction that things can and will be different, ultimately locates itself in the world through the decentered subjectivity of its participants. Education's hope is ultimately located in the world yet simultaneously remains outside of the causal structure of history. Through the inspiration to hope, education is located in an *ethical* space, a space of non-indifference to the marginalized and vulnerable other. In this space, education instantiates an ethical relation to the other others in the world yet beyond the pale of causality, outside of its jurisdiction. Inspiration is education's ethical animation to create a breach in the determinism that seems cognitively to have control of the world.

This final element of the ethical dynamics that give rise to education in formal schooling is the call of justice that comes from the world. To be educational, formal schooling cannot remain insulated from the world, abstractly ensconced in the purity of the theoretical knowledge of the disciplines and in the asymmetries of the teaching and learning relationships. Formal schooling is always embedded in society. Of course, this is already also the case when it is dominated by human capital development and the global economy. But the call of justice from the world gives the everyday activities that constitute schooling's commonplaces an ethical orientation. And it is the call of justice that completes the dynamic in which education fully emerges. Education that arises in formal schooling fully emerges only when schooling does not evade the call of justice that comes from the vulnerable of the world and the fragility of the earth. To be educational in its most complete sense is to be outwardly directed to human and other creaturely flourishing. Education becomes completely visible when formal schooling is responsible to and inspired by the call of justice.

References

Aquila, R. (1983). *Representational mind: A study of Kant's theory of knowledge.* Bloomington, IN: Indiana University Press.

Arendt, H. (1968). The crisis in education. In J. Kohn (Ed.), *Between past and future: Eight exercises in political thought.* New York: Penguin.

Benso, S. (2000). *The face of things: A different side of ethics.* Albany, NY: SUNY Press.

Bergo, B. (2005). What is Levinas doing? Phenomenology and the rhetoric of an ethical un-conscious. *Philosophy and Rhetoric, 38*(2), 122–144.

Biesta, G. J. J. (2004). The community of those who have nothing in common: Education and the language of responsibility. *Interchange, 35*(3), 307–324. doi:10.1007/BF02698880

Biesta, G. J. J. (2010). *Good education in an age of measurement: Ethics, politics, democracy.* Boulder, CO: Paradigm Publishers.

Caputo, J. D. (2012). Teaching the event: Deconstruction, hauntology, and the scene of pedagogy. In C. Ruitenberg (Ed.), *Philosophy of Education 2012* (pp. 23–34). Urbana, IL: University of Illinois Press/Philosophy of Education Society.

Chalmers, D. J. (1997). *The conscious mind: In search of a fundamental theory.* New York: Oxford University Press, USA.

Higgins, C. (2011). *The good life of teaching: An ethics of professional practice.* Oxford: Wiley-Blackwell.

Joldersma, C. W. (2005). Incarnate being and carnal knowledge: The caress beyond the grasp. In J. H. Kok (Ed.), *Ways of knowing: In concert*. Sioux Center, IA: Dordt College Press.

Joldersma, C. W. (2008). The importance of enjoyment and inspiration for learning from a teacher. In D. Egéa-Kuehne (Ed.), *Levinas and education: At the intersection of faith and reason* (pp. 43–55). London & New York: Routledge.

Joldersma, C. W. (2011a). Ernst von Glasersfeld's radical constructivism and truth as disclosure. *Educational Theory*, 61(3), 275–293. doi:10.1111/j.1741-5446.2011.00404.x

Joldersma, C. W. (2011b). Providential deism, divine reason, and Locke's educational theory. *Journal of Educational Thought/Revue de La Pensee Educative*, 45(2), 113–125.

Joldersma, C. W. (2013a). An ethical Sinngebung respectful of the non-human: A Levinasian environmental ethic. *Symposium: Canadian Journal of Continental Thought*, 17(1), 225–246.

Joldersma, C. W. (2013b). Neuroscience, education, and a radical embodiment model of mind and cognition. In C. Mayo (Ed.), *Philosophy of Education 2013*. Urbana, IL: Philosophy of Education Society & University of Illinois Press.

Kant, I. (1996). Groundwork of the metaphysics of morals. In M. J. Gregor (Trans.), *Practical philosophy* (the Cambridge edition of the works of Immanuel Kant). Cambridge: Cambridge University Press.

Kant, I. (1999). *Critique of pure reason*. (A. W. Wood, Trans., P. Guyer, Ed.). Cambridge: Cambridge University Press.

Labaree, D. F. (2010). *Someone has to fail: The zero-sum game of public schooling*. Cambridge, MA: Harvard University Press.

Lakoff, G., & Johnson, M. H. (1980). *Metaphors we live by*. Chicago, IL: University Of Chicago Press.

Lakoff, G., & Johnson, M. H. (1999). *Philosophy in the flesh: The embodied mind and its challenge to western thought*. New York: Basic Books.

Levinas, E. (1969). *Totality and infinity: An essay on exteriority*. (A. Lingis, Trans.). Pittsburgh, PA: Duquesne University Press.

Levinas, E. (1985). *Ethics and infinity*. (R. A. Cohen, Trans.). Pittsburgh, PA: Duquesne University Press.

Levinas, E. (1987). *Time and the other*. (R. A. Cohen, Trans.). Pittsburgh, PA: Duquesne University Press.

Levinas, E. (1995). *The theory of intuition in Husserl's phenomenology.* (A. Orianne, Trans.) (2nd edition). Evanston, IL: Northwestern University Press.

Levinas, E. (1996). *Basic philosophical writings.* (A. Peperzak, S. Critchley, & R. Bernasconi, Eds.). Bloomington, IN: Indiana University Press.

Levinas, E. (1998a). *Discovering existence with Husserl.* (R. A. Cohen, & M. B. Smith, Trans.). Evanston, IL: Northwestern University Press.

Levinas, E. (1998b). *Entre nous: Thinking-of-the-other.* (M. B. Smith, & B. Harshaw, Trans.). New York: Columbia University Press.

Levinas, E. (1998c). *Of God who comes to mind.* (B. Bergo, Trans.). Stanford, CA: Stanford University Press.

Levinas, E. (1998d). *Otherwise than being: Or beyond essence.* (A. Lingis, Trans.). Pittsburgh, PA: Duquesne University Press.

Levinas, E. (1998e). The ruin of representation. In R. A. Cohen, & M. B. Smith (Trans.), *Discovering existence with Husserl* (pp. 111–121). Evanston, IL: Northwestern University Press.

Levinas, E. (1998f). Uniqueness. In M. B. Smith, & B. Harshaw (Trans.), *Entre nous: Thinking-of-the-other* (pp. 189–196). New York: Columbia University Press.

Levinas, E. (1999). *Alterity and transcendence.* (M. B. Smith, Trans.). New York: Columbia University Press.

Levinas, E. (2001a). *Existence and existents.* (A. Lingis, Trans.). Pittsburgh, PA: Duquesne University Press.

Levinas, E. (2001b). *Is it righteous to be?* (J. Robbins, Ed.). Stanford, CA: Stanford University Press.

Levinson, M. (1999). *The demands of liberal education.* New York: Oxford University Press, USA.

Llewelyn, J. (2004). *Seeing through God: A geophenomenology.* Bloomington, IN: Indiana University Press.

Lynch, M. P. (2001). *Truth in context: An essay on pluralism and objectivity.* Boston, MA: MIT Press.

Merleau-Ponty, M. (1962). *Phenomenology of perception.* London: Routledge & Paul.

Panksepp, J. (1998). *Affective neuroscience: The foundations of human and animal emotions.* New York: Oxford University Press, USA.

Schwab, J. J. (1978). *Science curriculum, and liberal education.* Chicago: University of Chicago Press.

Spring, J. (2008). *Globalization of education: An introduction.* London & New York: Routledge.

Thompson, E. (2010). *Mind in life: Biology, phenomenology, and the sciences of mind*. Cambridge, MA: Belknap Press of Harvard University Press.

Tuschling, A., & Engemann, C. (2006). From education to lifelong learning: The emerging regime of learning in the European Union. *Educational Philosophy and Theory, 38*(4), 451–469. doi:10.1111/j.1469-5812.2006.00204.x

Wilson, F. R. (1999). *The hand: How its use shapes the brain, language, and human culture*. New York: Random House.

Wolterstorff, N. (2004). *Educating for shalom: Essays on Christian higher education*. (C. W. Joldersma, & G. G. Stronks, Eds.). Grand Rapids, MI: Eerdmans Publishing.

Zuidervaart, L. (2004). *Artistic truth: Aesthetics, discourse, and imaginative disclosure*. Cambridge: Cambridge University Press.

Index

adequation, 27, 46, 70
affective disruption, 10, 21, 115
agency, 28, 31, 33, 37, 68
ambiguity, 31, 79
Arendt, Hannah, 106
asymmetry, 14, 31, 34, 37, 44, 50, 57, 88, 97, 117
autonomy, 5, 44, 52, 110

Bergo, Bettina, 9
Biesta, Gert, x, 8, 47
bodies, 30, 82, 86

call, 4, 7, 12, 13, 14, 105
Caputo, John, 11, 18
caress, 79
centeredness, 20, 31
Chalmers, David, 44
classroom, 41, 58, 102, 108, 115
cognition, 35, 38, 76, 77, 79, 84
cognitive intentionality, 38, 64, 70, 75, 85
commonplaces, x, 4, 23, 90, 115
comprehending, 27, 46, 78
conditions
  ethical, 24, 31, 113
  for autonomy, 31
  for cognition, 71
  for education, 107
  for learning, 33
  for teaching, 44
  saying, 37
  time unforeseen, 39

conditions for learning, 32
consciousness
  and autonomy, 25
  enjoyment, 67
  hypostasis, 44
  intentionality, 26
  totality, 84
curriculum
  and touch, 81
  commonplace, 2, 62, 90
  content, 5, 62, 92, 93
  encyclopedic claims, 86
  ethical orientation, 81, 114
  representational, 70, 102
  subjects, 62
  unity, 86

disciplinary knowledge, 5, 41, 43, 64, 84, 95, 103, 108
disruption, 10, 32, 39, 47, 54
domestication, 14, 21, 45
dwelling, 29, 33, 36

earth, 3, 72, 117
education
  and justice, 3, 90, 103, 105, 117
  Arendt, 106
  emergence of, 2, 92, 107, 115, 117
  hope in, 108, 110, 116
emotions, 25
encounter, 49, 50, 83, 94, 98
Engemann, Christoph, 3

enjoyment, 35, 40, 45, 51, 66, 67
ethical
  first-person responsibility, 100
  nature, 42, 53
  obligations, 52, 56, 92, 99, 104
  relation, x, 23, 31, 34, 37, 38, 48, 57, 99, 105, 117
  relationship, 31, 37, 98, 102
  responsibility, 41, 91, 101
  spaces, 38, 102, 116
  undercurrent, 8, 96
ethical orientation, 2, 5, 24, 90, 112, 115, 117
ethics
  care-theory, 2
  deontological, 2
  disruptive, 5, 89
existence, 13, 35, 55
  bare existence, 35
  existent, 13
  mystery of, 13
experience
  ethical, 113

flourishing, 18, 21, 55, 74, 87, 113, 117
  bringing human, 111
  sustainable, 2
formal schooling, 5, 8, 23, 24, 57, 62, 89, 93, 104, 113, 117
  as education, 110
  hope in, 109
freedom, 15, 110

glory, 77, 81, 87
Good Samaritan, 105
grades, 56, 97
  grading, 91, 97
  justifying, 96
gratitude, 107

hearing, 52, 76, 81, 82
heteronomous relationship, 32, 47
Higgins, Christopher, 55
high-stakes testing, 8
hope
  affective disruption, 116

and action, 108, 116
and curriculum, 88
and learning, 39
and tactful touch, 79
and the impossible, 19
and time unforeseeable, 11
as affective disruption, 10
as gift, 108
as response, 18
as trace, 17
for justice, 114
in education, 110, 116
inspiration to, 2, 4, 113
non-indifference, 20
student's, 33
teacher's, 60
horizons, 18, 72
  implicit, 73
  implicit bodily, 73
  unsuspected, 65
hospitality, 33, 37
  shelter, 36
  sheltering interiority, 46
  welcoming, 34
human flourishing, 4, 116

incomparables, 104
independence, 29, 30
inspiration
  as trace, 10
  beyond vision, 17
  condition for learning, 28
  disrupts learning, 39
  enigmatic, 11, 108
  ethical, 58
  ethical animation, 31
  external, 39
  formal, 40
  grounds learning, 34
  non-indifference, 116
  orients learning, 34
  primordial, 37
  subjectivity, 29
  to hope, 9
  transcendent condition, 16
  unforeseeable future, 18

Institutionalized education, 91
institutions, 3, 4, 51, 57, 115
intentionality, 27, 46, 69, 70
   conscious, 69
   directed activity, 68
   grasping, 68
   intentional arrow, 38
   of consciousness, 45
intentional relation, 70
intentional structure, subject-object, 73
interiority, 37
intersubjective, 2

Johnson, Mark, 68, 69
Joldersma, Clarence, 27, 29, 66, 75, 77
joy, 19, 28, 35, 45, 59, 67, 74, 116
justice
   and consciousness, 100
   and education, 3, 105, 111, 115
   call of, 4, 80, 91, 103, 112, 117
   delayed, 19
   hope for, 59, 114
   in classrooms, 102
   in curriculum, 103
   of life-giving disclosure, 90
   third party, 99

Kant, Immanuel, 25, 45
knowledge
   and autonomy, 25, 70
   and curriculum, 81
   and humanities, 63
   and trusteeship, 103
   and truth, 79
   as power, 74
   as property, 29, 46, 70
   body of, 46, 63, 96
   conditioned, 83
   constructivism, 27
   domesticating, 74
   encyclopedic, 84
   grasping, 54, 92, 114
   relativized, 81
   representationalist, 41
   teacher's subjectivity, 46
   totalizing, 85
   traditional view, 24

Lakoff, George, 68
learner
   and curriculum, 114
   and enjoyment, 37
   and hospitality, 33
   and time unforeseen, 32
   as autonomous subject, 26
   as other, 51
   autonomous, 26
   called, 41
   conscious subject, 26
   decentered, 38
   heteronomous, 28
   inspired, 31
   relation to teacher, 23
   saying, 37
learning
   and autonomy, 25
   and calling, 40
   and curriculum, 65
   and freedom, 26
   and hope, 39
   and hospitality, 113
   and representations, 26
   and transcendence, 23
   and world, 114
   commonplace, 2
   constructivism, 26
   double asymmetry, 114
   ethical orientation of, 23
   from a teacher, 27, 32
   hospitality, 33
   in school, 8
   inspired, 34
   intentionality, 26
   listening, 36
   risk, 38
   subject, 26
Levinas, Emmanuel, 2
Levinson, Meira, 24
life-giving disclosure, 80
listening, 115

memory, 13, 17, 52, 65, 77, 107
mental representations, 15, 26, 41, 46, 63
Merleau-Ponty, Maurice, 78
metaphors, 12, 16, 29, 33, 79, 85, 94
mind, 11, 64, 77

neighbor, 15, 41, 50, 53, 100
Noddings, Nel, x
non-representational relations, 80, 81
normativity, 9, 10, 105
nourishment, enjoyable, 66

obligation
    and education, 107
    asymmetry, 14
    passivity, 14
    to curriculum, 95
    to students, 48, 91, 96
openness, 28, 109
    and subjectivity, 30

Panksepp, Jaak, 73
passivity, 13, 80, 85, 116

representationalism, 74, 85
representational knowledge, 5, 61, 62, 66, 70, 74, 77, 88
representations
    and constructivism, 26
    and curriculum, 64, 70
    and power, 75
    and sensibility, 73
    and touch, 79
    as intermediaries, 63
    as partial, 86
    cognitive, 73
    cognitive intentionality of, 69, 72, 84
    disciplinary, 83, 102
    freedom, 70
    grasping, 45
    human, 76
    implicit horizons of, 72
    intentional, 37, 76
    intentionality, 73
    present, 11, 82

standard, 94
successful, 70
truth, 79
responsibility
    and face, 52
    and inspiration, 41
    and justice, 101, 114
    and society, 107, 109, 114
    and trusteeship, 82, 94, 114
    as call, 15, 96
    as normativity, 14
    call to, 2, 4, 92, 98, 102, 108
    enigma of, 15, 104
    felt, 13, 49, 92, 105, 109, 113
    limitless, 57, 93
    limits on, 95, 97, 104
    normativity, 92
    passivity of, 53
    teacher's, 52, 93, 103
    time immemorial, 41
    to act, 40
risk, 109

sameness, 47, 92
saying, 4, 25, 29, 38, 98
schooling, 2, 3, 8, 54, 58, 60, 64, 71, 85, 90, 91, 101, 105, 115, 117
Schwab, Joseph, 2, 90
self, 20, 33, 45, 64, 70
sensibility, 26, 73
singularity, 49, 50, 97, 105
sovereignty, 31, 77, 85
subject
    and freedom, 20, 30, 67
    and the other, 30
    autonomy, 24, 31, 70, 85
    bodily, 28, 71
    centered, 29
    cognitive, 26, 47, 69, 72
    conscious, 28, 67
    conscious subject, 14, 27, 46, 68
    decentered, 38
    embodied, 72
    enjoying, 35, 45, 66
    heteronomous, 31

subject—*Continued*
  hypostatic, 36
  independence, 67, 77
  independent, 45, 66, 75
  inspired, 21, 80
  passive, 76, 79
  responsible, 74
  self-preserving, 29
  student as, 32, 39, 64
  teacher as, 49
subjectivity, 5, 66, 75, 116
  and the other, 30
  as exposure, 30
  deep, 15, 75, 116
  freedom, 20, 70
  heteronomous, 28
  primordial, 27, 74
  radical intersubjectivity, 28

teacher
  and curriculum, 64, 82
  and hope, 60
  and justice, 102
  and time immemorial, 52, 75
  as other, 4, 22, 113
  as trustee, 83, 93, 103, 115
  as unforeseen, 39
  as unique, 48
  autonomy, 44, 47
  called, 52, 57, 114
  conscious subject, 47
  felt responsibility, 49, 51, 91
  freedom, 47, 51
  grading, 96
  inspired, 59
  learning from, 27, 32
  subjectivity, 5, 43
  welcoming, 33

teaching
  commonplace, 2
  ethical orientation, 115
  relation, 51
the face, 16, 41, 45, 58, 65
the hand, 35, 69, 113
the other, 2, 41, 75, 90, 117
  otherness, 39, 59, 75
third party, 40
Thompson, Evan, 44
time
  anticipations, 72
  Arendt, 106
  lag, 77
time immemorial, 4, 7, 17, 41, 52, 113, 115
time unforeseen, 4, 7, 113
totality, 32, 84
touch, 65, 115
  tactful, 5, 62, 115
  touching, 82, 87
trace, 10, 114
transcendence, 4, 9, 10, 12
transcendent conditions, 5, 14, 17
trustee, 83, 114
  disciplinary, 83
truth, 54

vision, 11, 20, 33, 59, 72, 76, 80, 85, 107
vulnerability, 21, 30, 35, 38, 41, 50, 54, 67, 74, 109, 116

Walhof, Darren, x
Wilson, Frank, 68
Wolterstorff, Nicholas, x

Zuidervaart, Lambert, 80, 87

GPSR Compliance
The European Union's (EU) General Product Safety Regulation (GPSR) is a set of rules that requires consumer products to be safe and our obligations to ensure this.

If you have any concerns about our products, you can contact us on

ProductSafety@springernature.com

In case Publisher is established outside the EU, the EU authorized representative is:

Springer Nature Customer Service Center GmbH
Europaplatz 3
69115 Heidelberg, Germany

www.ingramcontent.com/pod-product-compliance
Lightning Source LLC
LaVergne TN
LVHW041956060526
838200LV00002B/33